DECORATIVE BOXES

DECORATIVE BOXES
To create, give and keep

Juliet Bawden

Photography by Jan Baldwin

NEW HOLLAND

For Loveday Bawden

First published in 1993 by Letts of London,
an imprint of New Holland (Publishers) Ltd
London · Cape Town · Sydney

This paperback edition first published 1995

Copyright © 1993 Juliet Bawden

ISBN 1-85238-416-6 (hbk)
ISBN 1-85238-549-9 (pbk)

A CIP catalogue record for this book is available
from the British Library.

New Holland (Publishers) Ltd
Chapel House, 24 Nutford Place
London W1H 6DQ

'Letts' is a registered trademark of
Charles Letts & Co Ltd

Designed and edited by
Anness Publishing Ltd
Boundary Row Studios
1 Boundary Row
London SE1 8HP

Editorial Director: Joanna Lorenz
Project Editor: Lindsay Porter
Designer: Pedro Pra-Lopez, Kingfisher Design
Photographers: Jan Baldwin and Viv Yeo
Stylist: Tuula Whitlow

Typeset by MC Typesetting Ltd, Rochester, Kent

CONTENTS

INTRODUCTION

When I told friends that I was writing a book about boxes, their instant reaction was surprise, and then almost without exception they said 'Oh I've got a box which may interest you'. Nearly everyone owns a box of some kind or other because most people have possessions which need to be kept together somewhere – and that is frequently in a useful box that fits the purpose perfectly.

If you fall into this category, you may find you enjoy boxes as intriguing objects in themselves, and you may wish to create, as well as collect them. There are boxes to make and embellish in this book using almost every conceivable material. Some of the projects use traditional techniques, such as lacquer, decoupage, gesso and gold leaf. There are Victorian crafts like tinsel painting and shell boxes; thrifty projects using recycled materials – a scrap box and a papier mâché box; and there are the New World techniques of beaten tin, crackle glaze and naive painting.

As well as projects for you to make, I mention types of box that you might like to collect and offer some hints on how to keep and clean different types of box. Whether you are interested in boxes made by contemporary craftsmen, or in simple ones made from cardboard, or in ever more complicated mosaic boxes, I hope that you find box-making fun – and that you enjoy reading and using this book.

Juliet Bawden

A BOX FOR EVERY PURPOSE

The most versatile of storage items can be put to hundreds of different uses, and is often custom-made to suit particular requirements. There are fabric-lined boxes with compartments to hold anything from cutlery to mathematical instruments; exquisite needlework boxes containing all the tools of the dressmaker's trade; hat boxes, pill boxes, trinket boxes and more. Skilled craftsmen and women continue to make elaborate and beautiful pieces today, using every medium or decorative motif available. Individual as these pieces are, they still serve their primary function – to store and protect cherished objects.

Historical boxes

Whatever their shape, size or material, boxes are intrinsically useful items, which have usually been made to satisfy a purpose. Most types of box have been developed over the years simply because a container was needed to hold a product of some sort, and a box best answered this requirement. Although they can be highly decorated and visually appealing, boxes are also popular with collectors because they are functional. In particular, the majority of boxes, from large wooden chests to tiny metal tinderboxes, have a fascinating history.

ABOVE: A wooden box with an enamelled pewter lid in a design characteristic of Charles Rennie Mackintosh's style of Art Nouveau.

Chests, trunks or blanket boxes

The chest is the earliest example of a piece of furniture and it was originally used to store clothes, linen, documents or treasure. The first chests were small, portable and invaluable for people travelling from one place to another. Toilet chests of joined construction, with divisions for compartmentalizing articles, were made in Ancient Egypt. There is a fine example of a chest or large box in the British Museum, London, circa 1300 BC, which belonged to Tutu, wife of the scribe Ani, and which was removed from his tomb in Thebes. A slightly earlier dome-topped chest of wood coated with gesso (plaster) and painted with vivid war and hunting scenes came from the tomb of the Egyptian Pharaoh Tutankhamun (died *c.* 1340 BC) and is preserved in Cairo Museum.

As often happens throughout history, the skills of the ancients were lost through the ages. The first form of medieval chest or box in Britain dates from the fifth century AD and is a crude hollowed-out log fitted with a lid. Boarded and painted chests developed over the years and were often in the form of large rectangular boxes with a hinged lid. These were sometimes fitted with a lidded box at one end to accommodate sweet-scented herbs.

Progressive refinements were made to the basic form up until the end of the seventeenth century when the chest was replaced by a chest of drawers. Large lidded chests continued to be used throughout the eighteenth century for storing blankets and linen and there has been a revival in these large storage boxes during the 1980s and 1990s.

The most sought-after version of the chest is perhaps the nineteenth-century seaman's or captain's chest. These chests were made in many sizes, and were frequently constructed of camphor wood. They were used as storage on board clipper ships, and had to be very sturdy to withstand rough crossings. Because of this outstanding craftsmanship, many fine examples still exist today.

*LEFT: This small chest is
decorated with a painting
of an old clipper at sea
on the lid front.*

*LEFT: A modern trunk is
given an old-style
treatment, painted in a
folk art design by
Stewart Walton.*

RIGHT: A collection of Shaker boxes. The stackable oval boxes are beautifully made with overlapping joins. The candle box on the wall is made of punched tin.

Food and utensils

Before the advent of packaging and refrigeration, it was essential that food be stored in protective receptacles to keep it away from mice or other infestations. Grain and other food staples were stored in large boxes and barrels in the pantry, while smaller amounts of precious items such as tea, coffee and spices would be kept in the kitchen. Prosperous households with collections of silver and fine china would often have wooden or leather velvet-lined boxes and canteens to

store and protect precious items. These were specially made with individual compartments for each item to prevent them from knocking together or tarnishing.

As early as the 1790s the Shaker community in the United States started making distinctive lidded pantry boxes in different sizes for storing food. The lapped joints or 'fingers' used to make up the boxes are characteristic of Shaker craftsmanship. After the mid-nineteenth century these boxes were mass-produced in factories, and the style has enjoyed a resurgence in popularity today. The 'firken' was another distinctive design made by the Shakers in New Hampshire. This was circular, with a wire handle and wooden grip, and was made especially for storing apple sauce.

Communities have often produced boxes specifically for one type of food: in Sweden a large, shallow round box with a lid was used for storing layers of crispbreads, while in the United States wooden boxes in a variety of sizes were

BELOW: Tin boxes have been used for storing dry goods since tins first started to be used for packaging. They are practical and air-tight, and have the advantage for manufacturers of being a durable form of advertising.

produced for measuring grain. The practice was so widespread that these were produced commercially, and during the early nineteenth century manufacturers were required to stamp their name on the base of their boxes to guarantee the accuracy of their measures.

Many antique kitchen boxes still continue to serve their original purpose. Old pantry boxes and tins that have not been allowed to rust can still be used for storing dry goods. Many tea caddies are still in use generations after they were first constructed.

ABOVE: Boxes for the dining room are used to hold and protect china plates, two nut crackers, a grape vine trimmer and a set of cocktail sticks.

Tea caddies

The term tea caddy originally applied to porcelain jars imported from China that were used as receptacles for tea. Caddy is a corruption of the word 'kati', a Malay word used to describe a weight of 605g (1⅓lb).

During the eighteenth century the term tea chest was also used. The English furniture designer, Thomas Chippendale, specified that tea chests should be brass or silver. However, other materials were also used to make them, including copper, pewter, and tortoiseshell veneered onto wood. The ultimate form of tea caddy was a casket or box, with a hinged lid and a lock, usually made of mahogany, rosewood, and occasionally satinwood.

Salt boxes

It is difficult to tell exactly when the first salt boxes were invented because they have been used in kitchens for centuries. Salt was always a precious commodity, derived either from sea water or from underground mineral deposits. When used for cooking, salt was usually kept in a rectangular wall box near the fireplace, where it would keep dry. In England, salt boxes were usually made of oak, while in the United States they tended to be made of pine or maple. Because salt is corrosive, metal nails were seldom used in the manufacture of salt boxes. Instead, boxes were constructed using joinery or wooden dowels. Modern salt boxes, in fact, are often glued at the joints.

Most salt boxes have a sloping lid, and the back of the box, which stands slightly proud of the front, has a hole in it so that the box can be hung on the wall. Sometimes salt boxes are made of Tunbridge ware, and they are frequently painted in bright colours with a simple stylized pattern, such as a tulip, often found in European folk art.

Tinderboxes

Before the invention of friction matches, and their wholesale use from between 1830–40, the portable tinderbox was as ubiquitous as the twentieth-century cigarette lighter. Made from brass or iron, some tinderboxes were for household use alone, while others were small and compact so they could be slipped into a pocket. The box contained flint and steel and a supply of tinder. This was either a wad of charred linen or 'touchwood'. The flint was struck against the steel and the resulting sparks ignited the tinder which was then blown into a flame.

Tobacco boxes

Ever since the introduction of tobacco into Europe in 1565, boxes have been made to contain it. The most essential requirement of such boxes is that they maintain a constant level of humidity which preserves the aroma and texture of the tobacco.

The first tobacco containers were jars made in glazed earthenware. One of the most popular designs was delft blue and white china. These particular jars were made by many Staffordshire factories between 1840–1870 and were normally cylindrical with a removable lid.

*LEFT: Set of smoking
boxes, including snuff
boxes, cigarette boxes in
wood and silver and a
silver vesta matchbox
complete with a match.
Snuff boxes are now very
collectable as they are
small, easily stored and
reasonably priced.*

At this time, both tobacco jars and boxes were also being made from lead, pewter and brass. The lead varieties were used mainly in the home, while the brass and pewter boxes were intended for pocket use. Lead tobacco boxes date back from the middle of the sixteenth century, and were particularly popular from 1750–1870. Usually they were octagonal in shape and had a removable cover. They tended to have very little decoration but usually an interesting handle which depicted a famous figure of the day. A macabre but popular box in the nineteenth century was a coffin-shaped tobacco box.

Pocket tobacco boxes from Holland were frequently decorated with miniature versions of Dutch Old Masters. The English boxes of the same period are very plain in comparison, while those made in the United States were decorated with brightly coloured designs.

Cigarette boxes

It was not until cigarettes were manufactured on a commercial basis that special cigarette packets or boxes were made. The slide carton or box was manufactured for Wills's in 1892 in Bristol, England. These were an immediate success because they protected the cigarettes from being crushed. This was mainly due to the cigarette cards which, before they became collectors' items, were first introduced to stiffen the boxes. By 1900, cigarette cartons were mass-produced in Europe and the United States by individual factories on contract to tobacco companies.

From about the 1920s, when it became socially acceptable for women to smoke, decorative cigarette boxes began to appear. These were made from a range of materials including leather, lacquer, silver and enamel. Particularly beautiful are those which date from the Art Deco period.

Writing boxes and lap-tops

Writing boxes date back to when writing implements were first used. The monks of the Middle Ages used a box called a *scriptium* in which to keep their writing materials, and this was the ancestor of today's writing desk.

Originally, these boxes were mounted on stands and eventually on legs. Gothic boxes had lift-up lids that were hinged at the back. The tops were either flat or they sloped towards the front, providing a surface at an angle which could be used to lean on while writing, as well as acting as a cover for the writing implements inside. All these first boxes were for ecclesiastical, rather than domestic, use.

In time, a smaller, more compact box was needed for use at home and so lap-tops were developed. These were particularly popular during the nineteenth century when they were made in great numbers. The major advantage of the writing box was that individual members of a family could have their own place to store letters, inks, quills, paper, sand, wax and seals, all of which were required for letter-writing in those days. As they were portable, they could be used on a lap or at a table. Most lap-tops or writing desks are similar in that the top opens to

BELOW: Escritoire *or lap-top desk, inlaid with mother-of-pearl. These were very popular for centuries and were designed to hold stationery, ink, pens and nibs. On the underside of the lid is a compartment for storing letters.*

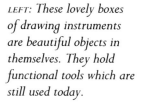

LEFT: These lovely boxes of drawing instruments are beautiful objects in themselves. They hold functional tools which are still used today.

ABOVE: A box containing an electric-shock machine. These were used from the end of the eighteenth century to the 1920s for curing all kinds of common ailments from colds and migraines to sore knees or rheumatism.

reveal a removable compartment tray for storing inkwells, pens, sand, seals and wax. Under the tray is a hinged folded surface for writing on, which is often covered in tooled leather, velvet or felt. A bottom compartment under the lid provides further space for storing papers and letters. Most lap-tops were made from wood or wood veneer, and they were sometimes inlaid with brass or ebony. Some lap-tops were personalized by having the initials of the owner inscribed on them.

Professional boxes

It is often the boxes of the professionals which are the most exciting – not necessarily because they are interesting on the outside, but because of the ingenious way these boxes have been constructed to protect their contents.

Often the box is as interesting and unusual as the items contained within it. Among the more extraordinary types of box for instance, are the electric-shock boxes which were popular at the

made today, with as much care and with the same excellent quality of materials as the boxes of yesteryear.

Less intricate, but just as useful are documents or deed boxes, originally used for protecting important papers from the elements. English deed boxes are the dull cousins of the painted American tin document boxes which abounded in the United States after 1810. These sturdy boxes can still be bought today, either new or secondhand. They still provide practical storage, and plain boxes are often collected and transformed with paint or decoupage.

Needlework boxes

One of the earliest examples of a sewing box found in the United Kingdom is an Anglo-Saxon circular bronze casket measuring 7.5cm (3in) high by 6.5cm (2½in) in diameter and which is displayed in the British Museum, London. The lid is unhinged and attached to the box by a short chain, and the top is decorated with a simple design in relief. The box would have been worn suspended from a belt or a girdle and would have contained needles and threads. From the earliest times, simple everyday items like pins and needles were scarce, difficult to obtain and highly valued, so it is not surprising that people carried them about their person. The British Museum box would have belonged to a woman of rank and status because it is made of bronze and very carefully decorated.

By medieval times, most ladies wore a needlecase of some sort attached to their girdles. It would usually have been made of bone or wood,

end of the nineteenth century and were used well into the 1920s for curing all kinds of ailments – from dislocated knees and deafness to the common cold. The older boxes were often made in a hardwood, such as oak, and had purple velvet linings and brass fittings.

The precision instruments of many professionals necessitated boxes with intricate compartments and linings – minute jewellers' weights and tweezers were carefully stored in sturdy wooden boxes with fabric-lined compartments for each item. These boxes continue to be

The needlework box played an important part in the nineteenth-century home. Normally 25–35cm (10–14in) long, 20–25cm (8–10in) deep and 20–23cm (8–9in) high, they were a convenient size to carry around or leave on a small table or chest of drawers. The boxes often held not only sewing implements but sometimes a piece of material which was in the process of being worked. These boxes were made of many different materials including mother-of-pearl, polished woods, and ivory. Boxes were also frequently inlaid or decorated with carvings.

LEFT: Two needlework boxes. The one on the left is from the 1820s. It is glass-topped with a picture of a woman in the dress of the period. Inside are small thimbles and other needlework tools.

though noble women had more elaborate silver ones studded with gems. As the art of needlework developed and new tools were invented, so needlework boxes changed. The fine cabinet and furniture-makers of the seventeenth and early eighteenth centuries were constantly seeking creative outlets for their skills and as domestic furniture came into its own so did needlework boxes. Gradually workboxes became subdivided with compartments for specialized accessories.

Games boxes

As long as people have been playing games, they have needed boxes to keep the elements of the game together. Horn is known to have been used for making containers for games as early as the Middle Ages. It was also used during the eighteenth and nineteenth centuries for making inexpensive copies of ivory boxes designed to carry dominoes, dice, and playing cards.

Some of the finest bone boxes were made by Napoleonic prisoners of war (1793–1815) who were allowed to make games and sell them for money to improve their living conditions. Chess pieces, draughts (checkers) and dominoes were made from bone as well as the boxes in which they came. From Regency times onwards, games compendiums were made to look like stationery and toilet boxes.

Jigsaws or dissected pictures, as they were first called, were invented in the nineteenth century. At first, the images were not very exciting and depicted such things as 'Queen

LEFT: A 1940s sewing basket complete with padded lining, skeins of darning wool and a darning mushroom.

RIGHT: Games boxes.
Clockwise from the back:
an original mah-jong set
with drawers to keep the
bamboo and ivory
counters; Ghanaian game
played with stones or
seeds; miniature dominoes
set; modern wooden box
for playing cards.

Victoria's Dinner at the Guild Hall with the Lord Mayor and Citizens of London, November 9th 1837.' The word jigsaw did not come into general use until the end of the nineteenth century when jigsaws took their name from the instrument which was used to cut the pieces. At first, jigsaws were sold in solid mahogany boxes with a sliding lid which carried a description of the puzzle inside and the maker's name. After 1850, mahogany boxes were replaced with varnished white wood, onto which brightly col-oured labels were stuck. By 1900 the old method of producing jigsaws with hand coloured engravings gave way to those with printed labels.

As more and more people had leisure time, so came the development of games. Particularly popular in Victorian times were boxes of cubes which doubled as six-sided jigsaw puzzles, with a different puzzle appearing on each side of the brick or cube. Often one of the pictures would also be shown on the lid of the box. The last 20 years have seen a revival in this kind of game.

Most toys are still sold in boxes, usually made of cardboard. Because of the fragility of the material used, in recent years boxes that are in good condition and which are 30 years old or more have become as much collectors' items as the toys contained within. Boxes which held model cars and vans are especially popular, and can fetch considerable sums of money.

Money boxes

In England the first money boxes were made of earthenware. Traditionally, a child's clay money box was made in the shape of a little pig – hence the name piggy bank. This form of box is universal to children all over the world.

Much later, Victorian children were encouraged to understand thrift and so attractive money boxes were produced in different shapes and sizes, and from many materials. These boxes came in the guise of cottages, shell boxes and even dogs' kennels. During the nineteenth century, Gorsty Hill of Worcestershire, England produced a very popular model known as the 'Hen and Chick' money box.

As copper coins increased in size, so did the size of the money boxes. The slit through which money is dropped can help a collector to identify the date of the box. For instance, eighteenth-century gold and silver coins were wafer thin, so the size of the hole through which they were dropped was small and narrow.

During the nineteenth century, there was a vogue for mechanical money boxes. Today, money boxes come in a wide range of materials and shapes, and they often depict popular children's fictional characters.

Advertising on boxes

The precursor of advertising on packaging can be traced to Roman times, when the shape of an earthenware pot indicated whether it contained wine or water. With wine, sometimes a mark would also be included to indicate from which vineyard it came.

By the eighteenth century, printed labels started to appear more frequently. They were not decorated at this time but by the end of the eighteenth century more elaborate designs were to be found on boxes for items as diverse as tobacco, pins and gloves. Often the label would be an extension of the manufacturer's trade card, which was printed from copper, steel and wood engravings. As techniques in commercial printing improved, so did the engraver's art. By 1850

LEFT: Three money boxes. The one at the top has a lift-out drawer and a secret compartment. The box on the left is a common design with an opening in the lid, while the box on the right has a less usual design, incorporating the slot in the side of the box.

colour printing was well established and a wide variety of designs were produced for drinks manufacturers in particular.

Victorian design was often ebullient, detailed, frivolous and colourful, so that early printed boxes must have stood out on the grocers' shelves. As manufacturers launched more and more products onto the market, the need to establish each brand's presence and image intensified. Much of this was done through advertising in books, magazines and posters. Before long, manufacturers had the dilemma of keeping their old-established designs or choosing to develop new ones. Throughout the twentieth century, many designs have been influenced by the prevailing artistic style of the day, and the art of the gallery filtered through to everyday life in the guise of advertising and packaging.

It was during the nineteenth century that the packaging of products developed quickly when inventors, mechanics and entrepreneurs collaborated to maximize the sales of their products.

Tin boxes were used in the first half of the nineteenth century for a number of perishable items, biscuits (cookies) in particular. Increased mechanization of biscuit (cookie) production in the 1850s produced a surplus which needed to be stored. Tin boxes were the best means of preserving them and stopping them from breaking. One British manufacturer, Huntley and Palmers, has used tins since the 1830s.

From the 1860s, it was possible to print directly onto tin. Offset lithography soon followed and the era of the Christmas biscuit (cookie) tin began. To increase sales at Christmastime, Victorian manufacturers made tins in a variety of shapes printed with decorative patterns. Popular designs included birds' nests, snakeskin and even rows of books.

The skill of cardboard box-making began at the turn of the nineteenth century in England, France and the United States when there was a huge demand for everything from small pill boxes to large hat boxes. By 1850 the firm of Robinsons of Chesterfield, England, advertised their ability to produce over 300 different shapes and sizes of box. The demand for cardboard boxes rose steadily but to succeed as an item cheap enough for grocery stores it needed to be mass-produced. The answer came in the form of

BELOW: Collection of boxes showing advertising slogans, including French and English soap boxes made from card and a tin cigarette box.

the folded carton which was made by cutting and creasing a single piece of card. The other advantage with cartons was that they took up very little room because they could be stored flat until they were needed. The first carton was made in the United States in around 1850 and was used for carpet tacks.

Dressing table and clothing boxes

For as long as people have been adorning themselves with clothes, accessories, jewellery and cosmetics, they have been constructing containers to put them in.

A Victorian dressing case or box could weigh as much as 9kg (20lb) with its full complement of fittings. Inside a beautifully lined and fitted box would be an array of silver-topped jars and bottles, containing all the luxuries used by the prosperous lady of the day: eau de cologne; lavender water; attar of roses; plus brushes, combs and a manicure set. Boxes such as these often included a secret drawer, which might have been used to store jewels or letters. They were often made of wood such as box or yew,

and may have been varnished and painted.

Hat pin, glove and handkerchief boxes would also be found on the dressing table. These were often dainty, prettily decorated items, covered in embossed paper or beautiful fabric, and edged with lace, not unlike the first commercially-produced Valentines.

Ornamental oval-shaped boxes known as band or bride boxes were used to store ribbons, or for transporting clothing and accessories, particularly men's collars and neckbands. These were made of lightweight, inexpensive materials such as card (posterboard) or pine, and were often decorated with wallpaper or decoupage. The hat box is a larger version of the band box, and can still be purchased today.

LEFT: Pretty boxes fit for a dressing table, including a box for handkerchiefs, hat pins, calling cards and a collection of pretty pill boxes in enamel, glass and metal.

BELOW: These unusual hat boxes are made from tin. The box on the left holds an officer's naval hat and the box on the right holds a top hat.

RIGHT AND BELOW:
Brightly coloured Peruvian hinged boxes, containing a miniature hat shop, a nativity scene, and tiny 'worry' dolls.

BOTTOM: Up-dated version of an old technique. These Russian trinket boxes have been painted and then given many coats of varnish.

Folk art designs

'Folk art' is an umbrella term for a vast range of artistic forms and utilitarian objects, ranging from primitive paintings and sculptures to furniture, kitchenware and other household items. The designs, motifs and decorative patterns range from brightly-painted Russian lacquer work to spare, unadorned Shaker designs.

Some of the most beautiful pieces of utilitarian folk art came from the religious settlements in the United States, where a disbelief in superfluous adornment resulted in clean, simple designs of breathtaking craftsmanship. From the second half of the nineteenth century, Shaker designs were produced commercially, and this style continues to inspire and delight today.

Russian folk art could not be more different than the subdued designs of the Shakers. Wooden artefacts are often decorated with brightly-coloured motifs of flowers and foliage. Like canal art, this technique involves direct

*LEFT: Two French boxes.
One is made from papier
mâché with a glass-topped
lid. The other is made
from wood and painted
with a floral motif.*

*BELOW LEFT: A miniature
chest decorated with folk
art motifs, just 10cm
(4in) tall.*

*BELOW: Russian lacquer
trinket boxes with
separate lids, decorated in
gold, red and black.*

painting onto the artefact without a preliminary
drawing. The pattern is executed with bold
brush strokes, with contours often executed in
white. This work was often carried out by
travelling craftsmen, which accounts for the
similarities in pieces produced in different vil-
lages. Many contemporary boxes and other
artefacts continued to be decorated in this style
and with a little practice the effect can be
re-created at home.

Contemporary boxes

There are many artists and craftsmen and women practising today who create boxes in a wide range of media. The price of these items will depend on the materials used and the extent of the work involved, but they are often reasonably affordable, and can be an excellent way to begin a contemporary craft collection. Many established artists show their work at craft fairs, so it is worth noting venues in your local entertainment listings. Art school degree shows are another good source of innovative work, and often provide the opportunity to support the artists of tomorrow. Many artists will also accept commissions.

LEFT: Three presentation boxes by Tricia Rafferty. Each box contains a porcelain figure. The decorations on the boxes complement the styles of the figures within.

BELOW: Three pill boxes by Tricia Rafferty, exquisitely decorated in miniature, both inside and out.

Disguised boxes

Boxes come in all shapes and sizes but conventionally they are geometric, and usually have a lid. This need not be the case, as the wonderfully innovative designs on these pages show. Sometimes a box is completely disguised, and it is only upon handling the item that it reveals itself to be a container. The Victorians, particularly, loved the idea of *trompe l'oeil* and disguised objects and produced secret boxes from items such as hollowed-out books or globes.

Modern craftsmen and women have taken up the challenge and continue to produce unusually-shaped boxes. The miniature boxes of Vicki Ambery-Smith are based on architectural models, whether Florentine Renaissance chur-

ches or the buildings of Inigo Jones. Sarah Parker-Eaton bases her miniature boxes and jewellery on insect forms, resulting in fabulous imaginary creatures.

Animals are a favourite theme for many designers, no matter what scale or material they work with. These may range from the big, bold wood carvings of Nicola Henshaw to tiny papier mâché fish boxes able to be concealed in the palm of one's hand. Animals may be used as a painted motif on a conventionally-shaped box, as a decorative handle, or as the form of the box itself. These are often beautiful and covetable items in their own right, with the added advantage of being practical containers.

BELOW: A soap-stone lion box. The lion shape lifts away from the base to reveal a cavity large enough to store trinkets or jewellery.

LEFT: Turned wooden boxes formed in the shape of an apple and pear. The box on the right is used as an ice bucket and is made from a real coconut.

OPPOSITE: Carved wooden jointed boxes by Nicola Henshaw. These superb boxes in the shape of a seagull, pelican and whale each contain a surprise — small carved fish, starfish, shells and seahorses.

RIGHT: *An enchanting collection of house boxes, made from card and tin. They are used for storing stationery, tea, candies and trinkets.*

OPPOSITE: *A ceramic box shaped like a hen, complete with black soap-stone eggs. This would be a delightful place to hide Easter eggs.*

BELOW: *Miniature boxes by Vicki Ambery-Smith, inspired by the architecture of Renaissance Florence.*

OPPOSITE: Boxes come in all forms. This charming collection of animals is made from different materials — the dove is of soap-stone, the hare of wood, the box with a turtle on the lid is woven, and the two birds are made from straw.

LEFT: All of a theme — a collection of small fish boxes. Clockwise from top: Indian papier mâché box; papier mâché fish box — one-off design made by pulp method; loose fish on top of small wooden painted box by Jill Hancock; octagonal box with fish design; fish box with wooden starfish inside, by Jill Hancock.

BELOW: Miniature metal boxes by Sarah Parker-Eaton, based on insect forms.

RIGHT: Customized shoe boxes by Julie Nock, decorated with decoupage cut-outs of the artist's own design. The shoe was made by the artist from plastic tubing.

OPPOSITE: Three modern boxes made from pulped papier mâché painted in vibrant colours by Kim Jefferies.

BELOW: Unusual ice boxes from Zimbabwe made from papier mâché decorated in vibrant acrylics.

OPPOSITE: Contemporary boxes with drawers made from recycled wood by Rachel Maidens.

BELOW: Clara Vicki is a jewellery designer who packages her work in these specially designed metal pill boxes.

LEFT: A collection of paper-covered boxes printed with animal motifs. One box with a handle becomes a suitcase; one is equipped with drawers to store small items. A narrow box in the foreground is used for storing postcards.

OPPOSITE: Catriona Stewart's range of pretty little trinket boxes are printed with watercolours and intimate messages both inside and out.

LEFT: Miniature boxes made of silver have been popular for years, as this collection of antique and modern boxes illustrates.

BELOW: Decoupage hat box by Emma Whitfield, and boxes inspired by fertility symbols and the lunar cycle by Barbara Stoddard. The base of the box in the background is inscribed with a Navaho Indian fertility poem.

CREATING BOXES

This section is full of ideas for creating unique but functional boxes for every purpose, and clear, step-by-step photographs will show you how it's done. There are painted boxes and stencilled boxes, boxes decorated with shells or mosaics, fabric-covered boxes and boxes made from recycled materials. Many of the techniques have a long pedigree – including lacquering, gilding, and punched tin – and others are quite unexpected – boxes made from machine-embroidered fabric, or even gingerbread! The techniques are all quite simple to master, and are sure to inspire your own creations.

Fabric Boxes

Fabric can be used for boxes in many ways. It may cover the box, be used as decoration, or form the basis of the box itself. The following projects include a box made from simple unbleached cotton, strengthened and decorated with machine embroidery, and a sophisticated box embellished with elaborate appliqué. There are also ideas for making wonderful storage containers by covering plain cardboard boxes with fabric, and edging them with braid, ric rac or ribbon. The ultimate luxury box has to be the soft sculpture chocolate box, with each individual chocolate sewn to look as tempting as the real thing, resulting in a wonderful visual feast.

ABOVE: Chocolate box by Deidre Hawken and Gudrun Luckett.

RIGHT :Machine-appliquéd box by Abigail Mill.

Fabric-covered boxes

A very simple yet effective way of creating storage boxes is to cover plain cardboard boxes, such as shoe or hat boxes, with fabric.

PREPARATION

MEASURING UP FOR A CIRCULAR BOX
You need a rectangle of fabric whose length is the circumference of the box times the width of the box plus 5cm (2in) for the bottom edge.

For the lid, place the box lid on the fabric and draw around it. Cut out the fabric, to lie just short of the lid's edge. For the edge of the lid, cut a strip of fabric 3 times the depth of the lid edge, and long enough to go around the lid.

1 ▲ Using fabric glue, stick the long rectangle of fabric round the box, making sure that one edge is aligned with the top of the box. You may use a piece of tape to hold the fabric in position.

LEFT: Fabric-covered boxes by Katie Scampton. A cardboard hat box and two shoe boxes are the bases for these handsome boxes. They have been covered in blue and white gingham and edged in braid or embossed ribbon to give a neat finish.

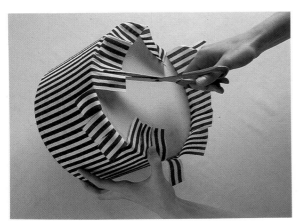

2 ▲ Snip into the excess fabric along the bottom edge at 2cm (1in) intervals.

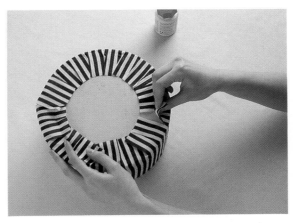

3 ▲ Spread glue on the bottom of the box to the depth of the overlap. Section by section fold the snipped fabric onto the glue and press down hard. Leave to dry for about 2 hours. ▶

Materials and equipment

- *cardboard box*
- *non-stretching, durable fabric such as cotton, canvas or hessian (burlap)*
- *ruler*
- *pencil*
- *dressmakers' scissors*
- *fabric glue*
- *tape (optional)*
- *cord (optional)*

4 Cover the lid by sticking the strip onto the outside edge so that there is as much fabric hanging below as above the side of the box lid.

Snip both the overhanging sides as you did at the bottom of the box, when covering the sides. Spread glue on the inside lip of the lid and stick down the snipped edge. Spread glue on the edge of the top of the box and stick down the other snipped edge.

5 ▲ Stick the circle of fabric on the outside top of the box covering the snipped edges. For a neater finish, cover the inside of the lid with a fabric circle slightly smaller than the lid size.

If you wish, punch holes in the sides of the box and add a cord handle.

MEASURING UP FOR A SHOE BOX

You will need 2 squares of fabric which measure the same as the narrow ends of the box allowing an overlap of 5cm (2in) to the width and 7.5cm (3in) to the depth.

For the sides of the box you will need 2 rectangles whose length is just short of the box and whose depth includes a 7.5cm (3in) overlap.

For the lid, you need a rectangle of cloth the same dimensions as the top of the lid plus double the depth of the sides of the box lid.

COVERING A SHOE BOX

1 Stick the end pieces of fabric onto the box first, making sure that the overlap is equal all the way round. Snip vertically into the corners of the overlaps. Spread glue to the depth of the overlap on the inner edge, base and two long sides of the box. Press the side edges in position first, then stick the top to the inside edge. Lastly, press the bottom edge to the base of the box.

2 When both ends have been glued, stick the fabric to the sides of the box, making sure that the overlap is equal. Spread glue on the inside edge of the box to the depth of the overlap, then turn in the fabric and stick down. Repeat with the bottom of the box.

3 Apply glue to the lid. Lay the fabric on your worktop with the wrong side facing upwards. Place the lid on top of the fabric with an equal amount of overlap all round.

4 Snip into the corners of the overlap. Spread the glue along the outside and inside edges of the box lid. Bring the fabric up the sides, fold it over the edges and press down.

LEFT: Machine-embroidered boxes by Linda Miller. These boxes are constructed solely from calico (cotton) and machine embroidery threads. The density of the stitches makes a very strong surface. The rayon thread gives a sheen to the whole box, which is then lined with silk.

Machine-embroidered box

This extremely unusual box is made from calico lined with silk. The box is not stiffened with anything other than the very dense machine embroidery. This simple design consists of flowers and leaves scattered with gold dots on a rich turquoise background. The top and bottom of the box are made in the same way, except that the sides of the lid are half the depth of the base. Also, the lid top has to be slightly bigger than the bottom so that it will close over it.

PREPARATION

If you are using a domestic sewing machine, the machine will need to rest every so often to stop the engine overheating. Before you begin, it is a good idea to practise on a spare piece of calico, to get the feel of the technique and to work out the tension you will need to use. Drop the feed dog teeth on the machine. With machine embroidery the fabric is moved by the use of an embroidery frame backwards and forwards, which is why you do not need a stitch length. Turn the stitch length to 0 and the width to 0. Hold the fabric taut in the embroidery hoop and work from the middle outwards. Try out and adjust the tension as necessary.

Note: Do not cut away the surrounding fabric until you have finished. The machine embroidery will seem to shrink the fabric and you need to leave room for adjustments.

Materials and equipment

- pencil
- paper
- scissors
- calico or cotton fabric
- sewing thread (silk rayon), selection of colours
- sewing machine with a darning foot
- embroidery hoop
- lining (pale pink silk dupion was used here)
- dressmakers' pins

1 ▲ Plan your design and pattern on paper. The more time you can spend experimenting with colours and motifs, the more likely you are to achieve a pleasing end result. Try unusual colour combinations and different shapes for the box.

2 ▲ Trace your chosen design onto paper and cut out. Use this as a template and draw each pattern piece onto calico in pencil. Leave a border around each piece as the embroidery will pull in the fabric and decrease the original dimensions.

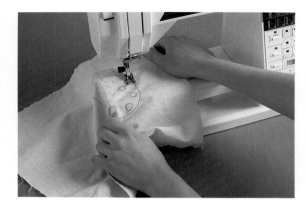

3 ▲ With the feed dog teeth of the sewing machine in their normal position, follow the pencil outline using a normal running stitch. When all the patterns have been stitched, prepare the machine for machine embroidery.

4 ▲ Place the calico in the embroidery hoop. Start the machine embroidery, working from the middle outwards. This will reduce puckering and bubbling. Keep the calico as tight as possible in the hoop.

5 Fill in the design as if you were painting, and remember to rest the machine when it gets hot. The embroidery will pull at the material so that it seems to shrink. If this happens too much, embroider a little extra at the sides. Cut out the embroidery, leaving a border of 1cm (⅜in).

6 When each section of the outer box is complete, measure and cut a piece of silk lining of the same dimensions. Machine-sew each lining onto the wrong side of the outer piece as close to the edges as possible using a running stitch. Once all the pieces are sewn, cover the running stitch with a close-set zigzag.

7 ▶ Twist a skein of coloured embroidery threads together. Stitch using a less close zigzag. Sew the twisted skein around each edge of the box. Pin the sides of the box edge to edge with the lid and the base. Over-stitch the sides to the lid and base by hand.

Machine-appliquéd box

Fabric panels have been used to cover boxes from as early as the seventeenth century when exquisite materials such as chenille were used and decorated with wire, beads, sequins and mica. The fascination with these boxes, especially those of the Stuart court, is that they give such a clear idea of people's interests at that time and also of the costumes worn then. Often these early embroidered boxes showed Old Testament scenes with landscapes crowded with animals, insects, birds, fishpools, mermaids, buildings and even rainbows.

Stumpwork (also known as raised work) was frequently incorporated in these early embroidered panels. This is a form of appliqué where, for instance, a silk background might be slashed and then filled with lambswool so that the front of the work is raised. Many different types of padding and stitching can be used. Unlike today, with the rise of the craftsmen and women who are designers and practitioners, the people who carried out these embroideries were rarely the designers. The designs usually came from professional designers and then young girls would carry out the embroidery and appliqué work as part of their needlework training. Many of the designs were taken from prints, woodcuts and engravings, which had not originally been intended for embroidery but were often book illustrations.

The box designed here as a project also depicts natural forms – those of shells. The use of rich fabrics such as chiffon, silks, organzas and metal organzas, and velvet results in a sumptuous box with stunning visual appeal. The Shaker-style box underneath forms a sturdy base

DESIGNING A MACHINE-APPLIQUÉD BOX

Although this box uses shells as a theme, the beauty of the design is as much to do with the rich fabrics used as with the motifs. The fabrics are arranged in layers, and then areas of the fabrics on top are cut away to reveal other fabrics beneath. Some areas are built up with felt, to make parts of the design more prominent than others. There are no rules; experiment with different materials to find out what achieves the most pleasing results.

PREPARATION

The box is made from two main side pieces, a lid, a band which goes round the rim of the lid and a piece of fabric to cover the base. Measure the circumference of the box and the depth of the lid and base. Draw a pattern to these dimensions, adding a 2cm (¾in) seam allowance.

LEFT: Machine-appliquéd box by Abigail Mill. This wooden box has been painted inside before being covered on the outside with machine-appliquéd panels in organza, silk, velvet and felt. The design is based on shell shapes.

1 Sand down the inside of the box with the sandpaper and wipe clean. Stain the inside with diluted acrylic paints. Sand off any excess, for a worn effect. Allow the paint to dry, then apply 2 coats of clear matt (flat) polyurethane varnish. Leave to dry.

2 ▶ For the main side bands, pin the pattern pieces onto 2 pieces of silk and 1 of organza, making 3 layers for each pattern piece. ▶

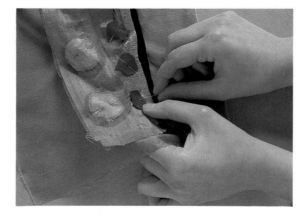

Materials and equipment

- *oval wooden box*
- *tape measure*
- *paper*
- *pencil*
- *fine-grade sandpaper*
- *acrylic paints*
- *paintbrushes*
- *clear matt (flat) polyurethane varnish*
- *brush, for varnishing*
- *pieces of silk, chiffon, organza, felt, velvet*
- *dressmakers' scissors*
- *fine scissors*
- *dressmakers' pins*
- *sewing machine*
- *needle*
- *thread*
- *thick wadding (batting)*
- *PVA (white) glue*

3 ▲ Sew the layers together, creating patterns with lines of running stitch. Using fine scissors, cut away some areas of the fabric to reveal those below. Cut the side band for the lid from a piece of velvet.

4 ▲ Pin a thin band of heavy fabric such as velvet to the wrong side of the embroidered side pieces to neaten the raw edges.

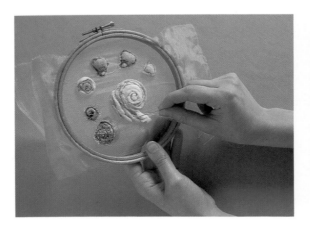

5 ▲ Decorate the lid by hand-sewing felt shapes stuffed with wadding (batting) onto a piece of organza. Pin a thin layer of wadding to the reverse side of the embroideries, and pin the lid band in place on the reverse side. Fit the lid piece over the box and sew in place.

6 Glue the base piece to the bottom of the box. Stretch and pin the main band round the base of the box. When it fits neatly and evenly, hand-sew or glue in place, unpinning and working with a little of the fabric at a time.

LEFT: Chocolate box by Deidre Hawken and Gudrun Luckett. They look real but they're made of fine fabrics, tissue lamé and organza decorated with beading and fine stitching. A wonderful box of 'chocolates' and a visual feast to give to your friends.

Box of chocolates

This tempting box of chocolates is almost a 3-D *trompe-l'oeil* – a visual feast as well as an amusing idea. The box is covered in a sumptuous fabric and filled with fabricated 'chocolate' shapes including a truffle, a caramel, and one with a violet petal.

Materials and equipment

- *clean, old nylon tights or stocking*
- *brown fabric dye*
- *stiff card (posterboard)*
- *scissors*
- *PVA (white) glue*
- *fabric such as silk satin, silk organza, fine silk, silk taffeta, red lamé, crushed velvet*
- *fabric glue*
- *piping (optional)*
- *25g (1oz) cotton mould*
- *rocaille beads*
- *needle and thread*
- *scalpel*
- *2.5cm (1in) thick foam*
- *string*
- *thin wadding (batting) (optional)*

PREPARATION

FOR THE 'CHOCOLATES'
Dye the silk organza and the fine silk brown. Follow the instructions on the pack for dyeing and fixing.

FOR THE CHOCOLATE BOX
You can either cover an existing box, or make up a new one as follows. Use stiff card (posterboard) for the box. You need 2 circles: 1 for the base 11.5cm (4½in) diameter and 1 for the lid slightly larger. Cut 1 strip of card 2cm (¾in) deep to make the lid of the box and cut another strip 3.5cm (1¼in) deep for the base. Stick the ends of the strips together, using PVA glue, so they form 2 rings. Cut 2 more circles, one to fit inside the box base and one to fit inside the lid.

Note: Based on these measurements, 7 chocolates will fit into the lid. These can vary in shape – round, oblong, square or oval, for instance.

1 ▲ Cover the card with the chosen fabric, sticking it in place with fabric glue. If you are using piping round the base and the lid, stick it on next. Then assemble the box and lid by sticking together with fabric glue.

2 ▲ To make the chocolate cases, cut a circle of silk organza at least 2.5cm (1in) in diameter (to fit all sizes of chocolates). Then pleat a strip of organza, about 2cm (¾in) deep, which is long enough to go round the circle. You may have to stick 2 pieces together. To pleat the fabric, wet it and iron it in pleats on a low heat. Stick it to the underside of the circle with fabric glue.

3 ▲ To make a truffle, cover a 25g (1oz) cotton mould (or cut foam into a round shape) in a piece of nylon and then sew on the rocaille beads at random.

4 To make a red caramel, use a sharp scalpel to cut a cube of foam about 2.5cm (1in) square. Cut a square of red lamé large enough to cover the cube. Sew with fine running stitch 3 small strips of string to the underside of the lamé to form ridges on the chocolate. Stick the lamé to the foam cube with fabric glue. You can make an empty foil wrapper by scrunching up a piece of lamé, and stitching lightly to hold.

5 ▲ To make a chocolate with a violet leaf, first cut a cube of foam about 2.5cm (1in) square. Cut a square of silk large enough to cover the top, which could be slightly padded with thin wadding. Then cut a strip of silk to go round the sides of the chocolate. Stick with fabric glue.

To make a crystallized violet, scrunch up a piece of wet silk taffeta about 2.5cm (1in) square and tie with string. When dry this will hold its shape. Cut the dried taffeta to the desired size and shape, and stick on top of the chocolate.

6 Stick the finished chocolates into the cases with fabric glue and then onto the box lid.

Paper Boxes

Paper boxes can be constructed from thick paper or thick cardboard, or may use paper to add the final embellishments. You may want to construct a beautiful and sturdy container out of papier mâché, or personalize an existing box using decoupage. There are some more unexpected ideas, too – including an extravagant-looking box for storing postcards or photographs, and a wonderful mixed-media drum box inspired by Native American and African motifs. The wonderful results belie the cost of the materials – all of the projects can be made fairly inexpensively, often with ordinary household items, and none of them require expert craft skills – just a little patience and imagination.

ABOVE : Papier mâché box with bird-shaped handle by Marion Elliot, executed in brilliant primary colours.

Hat box

Hat boxes are naturally wonderful for storing hats, but they can also be used for all kinds of things such as needlework supplies, beads and buttons, gloves or even socks. The box here is made from straw card (thin cardboard) and was obtained by mail order. It was decorated with a technique known as decoupage. This is a very simple and effective craft which requires little artistic ability and involves glueing cut-out paper shapes onto a surface, which is then varnished for protection. This method may be used to decorate boxes of any size or material – cardboard, wood or even metal.

LEFT: Decoupage hat boxes by Emma Whitfield. Decoupage is a boon for anyone who cannot draw but has a good eye for composition. The shapes are cut out and stuck onto a painted background. The whole box is then varnished and sanded many times for a lacquer-like sheen.

1 ▲ Paint the box with as many coats as necessary to give good coverage. Follow the manufacturers' instructions, allowing each coat to dry before the next. Depending on the finish you desire, you could use matt (flat) or silk (satin finish) paint instead of gloss.

2 ▲ Cut out the shapes required from the wrapping paper, using large scissors for wide areas and small nail scissors to cut out details.

Materials and equipment

- *1 large cardboard hat box*
- *gloss paint*
- *paintbrush*
- *printed wrapping paper*
- *scissors and nail scissors*
- *PVA (white) glue*
- *glue brush*
- *matt (flat) polyurethane varnish (optional)*

3 ▲ Position the cut-out pieces on the box to find a pleasing composition. You may want to draw the position in chalk so that you can replace the pieces exactly when glueing. Coat the back of each piece of paper with glue, and stick to the box ensuring the paper is flat.

4 ▲ Seal the box with a protective coat of varnish or PVA (white) glue and leave to dry.

RIGHT: *Papier mâché boxes by Marion Elliot. These two flamboyant boxes are simple in construction — made of papier mâché on a card base. They are extremely well executed and painted in the signature colours of the artist — brilliant red, egg yolk yellow and turquoise.*

Papier mâché box

Paper was invented by the Chinese in the second century AD and they are known to have worn helmets of papier mâché – a pulp of mashed paper and glue – during the Han dynasty (206 BC–AD 220). Papier mâché is known to have existed in Europe since the seventeenth century and was used for making snuff and tobacco boxes during the eighteenth and nineteenth centuries. In the United Kingdom at this time a whole industry was established around products made from papier mâché – Japan ware and architectural papier mâché.

Japan ware is the name given to small papier mâché artefacts, including many types of boxes, which were lacquered to give a black glossy finish, and often inlaid with mother-of-pearl. Architectural papier mâché refers to wall brackets, sconces and moulded ceiling ornaments which were all made from paper pulp. This was successful because it was a light, inexpensive material and replaced more expensive carving.

It is because the materials are inexpensive and easily available, and no special training or equipment is needed, that many people have turned to papier mâché as a means of creating artistic works. In many countries, papier mâché strongly features in folk art, and is often highly coloured, with simple yet effective designs. This project features bold colours with a simple motif.

DESIGNING A PAPIER MÂCHÉ BOX

A papier mâché box can be almost any shape and size. It can be made from an existing box onto which layers of papier mâché are added, or it can be made from chicken wire or plastic, covered in pulped paper or layers of glue and paper. The box could be finished with a smooth or deliberately uneven surface, or decorated with shells stuck onto the papier mâché, or cellulose filler squiggles, or whatever you wish. A cardboard papier mâché shape of a shoe or even a hamburger, fruit or flowers could be added to the top of the box. It is up to you how you use this versatile medium.

PREPARATION

Mix the wallpaper paste with water in a bowl. Tear the newspaper into strips running with the grain of the paper.

Cover your work area with newspaper – papier mâché is messy! Make a space in an airing cupboard or somewhere warm where the box can be put to dry between layers.

1 From corrugated cardboard cut 2 pieces 17.5 × 12.5cm (7 × 5in) for the lid and base, 2 pieces 15 × 10cm (6 × 4in) for the long sides, 2 pieces 10 × 10cm (4 × 4in) for the short side, and 1 piece 14 × 8.5cm (5½ × 3½in) for the rim of the lid. Cut small heart shapes for the sides and a dog shape for the lid. Seal all the pieces with diluted PVA and allow to dry.

2 ▲ To assemble the box, glue one long side in position on the base 1cm (⅜in) from the edge and hold in place with masking tape on both sides while drying. Glue the short sides, and then the other long side. When dry, remove the masking tape and replace with adhesive paper tape. Tape the motifs in position.

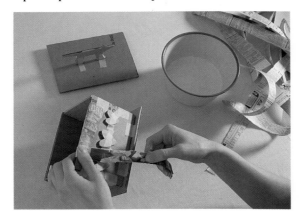

3 ▲ Cover the lid with 3 layers of pasted paper strips. Use small strips to evenly cover the dog handle. Put each layer on at a different angle so you can see where you have already layered. Apply 3 layers to the base of the box, using small strips of paper, and allow to dry for 2 days. ▶

Materials and equipment

- *wallpaper paste*
- *large bowl or bucket, for mixing wallpaper paste*
- *a good supply of newspapers*
- *38cm (15in) square of corrugated cardboard*
- *craft knife*
- *scissors*
- *PVA (white) glue*
- *masking tape*
- *adhesive paper tape*
- *paintbrushes*
- *white emulsion (latex) paint*
- *gouache paint in bright colours*
- *polyurethane varnish*

BELOW: Scrap box by Kirsty Rees. This rich-looking box is made for holding all those favourite postcards, or photographs destined for an album. Constructed from a corrugated card base, the frame is made from scrunched paper sprayed gold.

4 ▲ Apply 2 coats of emulsion (latex) to the inside and outside of the box. Allow to dry.

5 ▲ Draw the design on the box and paint in bright colours. Allow to dry then varnish to give a strong gloss finish to the project.

Scrap storage box

This box is inexpensive to make and involves recycling material. You can use any household scraps, including tissue paper, corrugated cardboard and pieces of string. When deciding how to design the box, consider what you might store in it and let this influence you. Although postcards are displayed on this box, other items would be just as suitable. For example, if you plan to store photographs in the box, use some to decorate the box sides. Diamanté, sequins and beads would be perfect for a jewellery box while old or foreign currency might be appropriate for a money box. Similarly, old maps would be good on a box for storing maps and an embroidered picture is ideal on a box for keeping embroidery threads. The options are endless.

Materials and equipment

- *5 favourite postcards or photographs*
- *ruler*
- *pencil*
- *craft knife*
- *corrugated cardboard pieces*
- *masking tape*
- *strong paper glue*
- *string*
- *tissue paper*
- *stapler (optional)*
- *gold or silver spray paint*
- *double-sided adhesive tape*

1 ▲ For the sides of the box, cut 2 equal-sized pieces of cardboard slightly bigger than the postcards. Cut the 2 end pieces, and the base according to the number of postcards you wish to store. Glue the edges of the box and hold with tape. Stick the base of the box onto the sides.

2 ▲ Cut 2 lid pieces slightly bigger than the base of the box and stick one on top of the other. Place the lid on top of the box and mark with a pencil where you will need to stick the rim edge. Cut 4 pieces of cardboard 1cm (⅜in) deep. Stick these on the underside of the lid.

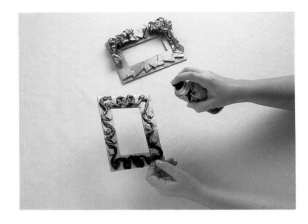

3 ▲ Out of more corrugated cardboard cut 4 frames the same size as the box sides and 1 the size of the box lid. Stick or staple twisted lengths of string and scrunched up tissue paper onto the frames. Spray the box, lid and frames with gold or silver paint. Leave to dry.

4 ▲ Attach the postcards to the underside of the frame using double-sided tape. Then stick the frames to the sides and top of the box with double-sided tape.

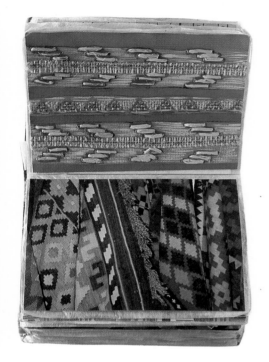

Recycled drum box

ABOVE RIGHT: Recycled woven boxes by Amanda Barry. These boxes are made from a variety of materials including corrugated card, sugar paper, yarn, and fabric.

ABOVE AND RIGHT: Pages from Amanda Barry's sketchbook showing the sources for her box designs, such as simple patterns, and combinations of colours and textures.

This drum box is constructed from many different materials including corrugated card. The use of tassels, appliquéd work and painted animal motifs provide variations in colour and textural contrast.

DESIGNING A RECYCLED BOX

The size and thickness of the materials used, and the way the box is constructed, dictate the need for bold imagery and colours to decorate this box. Anything too flowery would be lost. For inspiration, look at the simple and strong motifs found in much African work, or the work of the Navaho Indians of North America. Big bold tassels and over-stitching emphasize the box's rustic form.

PREPARATION

First, construct the base and sides of the box. Cut 2 circles of corrugated card with a diameter of 30cm (12in) for the base of the drum. Glue together for strength. Cut a long strip of card the same length as the circumference of the base to form the sides.

Along one edge of the cardboard strip, measure up 3cm (1¼in), draw a line and score along it. Cut out triangle shapes along the bottom 3cm (1¼in) of the strip. These cut-out triangle shapes allow the card to be folded into a circular shape. Glue the sides in place by folding the scored card so that the triangles stick to the bottom of the base. Hold the triangles in place with masking tape until they are completely dry.

Make and construct the lid in the same way with a diameter of 31cm (12½in) and a depth of 8cm (3¼in).

Materials and equipment

- *corrugated cardboard*
- *ruler*
- *pencil*
- *scissors*
- *craft knife*
- *PVA (white) glue*
- *masking tape*
- *2 strips of fabric, 94 × 21cm (37 × 8¼in)*
- *4 circles of fabric, 2 with a diameter of 31cm (12½in) and 2 with a diameter of 30cm (12in)*
- *2 strips of fabric, 8cm (3¼in) width (for the outside lid)*
- *2 strips of fabric, 4cm (1½in) width (for the inside lid)*
- *hessian (burlap)*
- *thick darning needle*
- *coloured yarns*
- *coloured paper*
- *acrylic paints*
- *paintbrushes*
- *thin needles*

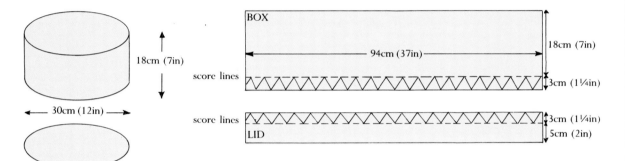

BOX
94cm (37in)
18cm (7in)
score lines
3cm (1¼in)

score lines
3cm (1¼in)
5cm (2in)
LID

18cm (7in)
30cm (12in)

1 ▲ Cover the cardboard drum and lid with fabric as for the Fabric-covered Box (page 42). Wrap the largest strip of fabric around the sides and glue in position. Repeat for the inside of the drum using hessian (burlap).

2 ▲ Pierce holes at regular intervals along the top edge of the drum using a thick darning needle. Sew along the top edge with coloured yarn, taking the yarn over the top using blanket- or over-stitching. ▶

3 ▲ Select yarns of different colours and thicknesses. For each colour measure 4 equal 18cm (7in) lengths of yarn. Take a long length of contrasting coloured yarn and bind each bundle of lengths in the middle to make a bow. Fold the bow in 2 and twist the remaining yarn round the top of the tassel and knot the 2 ends. Use the rest of the yarn to sew on the tassel.

4 ▲ You will need 8 animal motifs, 4 of the same design for the inside and 4 of the same design for the outside. Select coloured papers, thread, yarns and fabric. Using a pencil, draw the outline of the motif onto each square of coloured paper. Pierce the outline with a needle. Stick each piece of paper onto a piece of card the same size. This will help to stop the paper ripping when you are sewing. Sew round the motif using running stitch. Decorate the rest of the square with paper and paint.

5 ▶ Temporarily attach the motif squares on the outside of the box with masking tape. Carefully measure the distance between each square. Glue into place. Stitch on the tassels so that they hang on either side of the top 2 corners of the square. Repeat the measuring process with the inside of the drum and cover the tassel stitches on the inside of the drum with the motifs.

Wooden Boxes

The following projects include ideas for decorating wooden boxes, or for making your own, and you do not need expert woodworking skills to achieve fantastic results. Most of the constructed boxes are simply glued together, and decorated in bright, appealing colours. They include a miniature box containing a hidden surprise of wooden sheep, and an enchanting jack-in-the-box in bold primary colours. Decorating ideas include lacquering, gilding, naive-style folk painting and crackle-varnish, as well as an updated version of the traditional art of pyrography or wood-burning.

TOP: A colourful Jack-in-the-box, a perennial favourite with adults and children alike.

ABOVE: Lacquer box by Katie Scampton.

LEFT: Circus boxes. A wooden box with circus figures and animals; a clown box with a hinged lid; and a music box with a clown figure.

Jack-in-the-box

This traditional toy, thought to date from the early eighteenth century, has delighted generations of unsuspecting children. When the lid of the box is raised, the jack springs up to startle whoever has opened the box. Often the jack is a clown or jester with a red nose and sometimes with a prominent chin like Mr Punch.

Materials and equipment

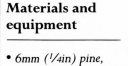

- *6mm (¹/4in) pine, 50cm (30in) long*
- *saw*
- *wooden block, 2.5cm (1in) square*
- *PVA (white) glue*
- *masking tape*
- *white emulsion (latex) paint*
- *acrylic paints*
- *paintbrushes*
- *small brass hinge and fixing screws*
- *bradawl*
- *screw-in hook and eye*
- *brightly coloured fabric*
- *needle*
- *thread*
- *dressmakers' scissors*
- *spring from an old-fashioned hair curler*
- *large wooden bead, 2.5cm (1in) diameter*
- *darning wool*
- *ribbon, 30cm (12in) long*

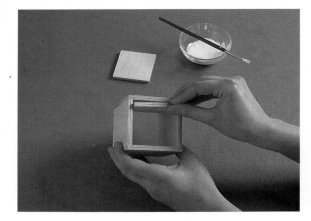

1 ▲ Cut out 4 sides, a lid and a base, 7.5cm (3in) square, plus a hinge support 6.2cm (2in) long and 1.25cm (1in) deep. Glue the 4 sides together into a box shape, then hold firmly in place with masking tape until the glue sets. Glue the hinge support in position. Glue the base of the box in position.

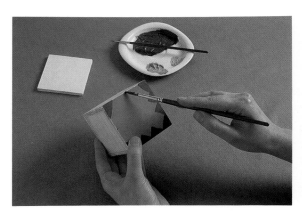

2 ▲ Paint the box with 2 coats of white emulsion (latex) and leave to dry. Paint the base colour with acrylic paints, leave to dry, then add the border decorations.

3 ▲ Add more details with acrylic paints and leave to dry.

4 Place the lid on top of the box, hold hinges in position and mark with a bradawl. Insert the screws and when they are all in position test the lid to see that it opens smoothly without jamming.

5 Put the eye into the middle of the front of the lid. Hang the hook from the screw eye and mark the position for the screw before inserting it. The box is now complete.

6 ▲ Cut a piece of fabric approximately 7.5cm (3in) wide, long enough to cover the spring, plus 1.25cm (½in). Sew a channel along one long edge and pass the thread through it. With right sides facing, fold the fabric in half and make a tube by sewing with running stitch. Turn the right way out so the seam is on the inside. Put the spring into the tube and draw the cord so that the end pulls tight over the spring.

7 Cut a wide-angled triangle of cotton in the shape of a hat. This can be the same material or different from that used on the body. With right sides facing and using a very tiny seam, sew along 2 sides to make a hat. Turn the right way out. Make the hair by loosely winding the darning wool around 4 fingers to make a tassel. Tie in the middle and trim the ends.

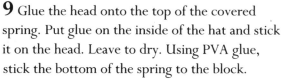

8 ▲ Paint a jolly clown face on the bead. Sew a length of ribbon with running stitches. Gather the ribbon to make a ruff. Tie the ends and glue round the neck. Glue the hair in position.

9 Glue the head onto the top of the covered spring. Put glue on the inside of the hat and stick it on the head. Leave to dry. Using PVA glue, stick the bottom of the spring to the block.

ABOVE: The Jack-in-the-box may be decorated in any style you choose.

LEFT: Jack-in-the-box by Jill Hancock. The Jack-in-the-box is the ultimate in surprises! This one is constructed using the spring from an old-fashioned hair curler. The bright colours and skilful craftsmanship make this appealing for all ages.

RIGHT: Decorative boxes by Jill Hancock. Small-scale boxes are decorated with bold patterns in strong colours. Each box contains simple stylized animal shapes which are integral parts of the design, and delightful toys in themselves.

Child's decorative box

Although this box could be for anyone, its bright cheerful colours and rural theme of grass and sheep make it ideal for a child. The sheep can stand on the surface of the box or can be kept inside, as a surprise. If you prefer, you can choose to decorate the box differently. For instance, you could make a handle from a small block of wood and glue it to the top of the box, or even use a large wooden bead or other wooden shapes.

You can make this box as large or as small as you wish. The dimensions here are roughly those of a box of kitchen matches – the smallness is part of its charm and children love miniature things. Because this is a very simple box to construct, it is a good one for a beginner. There are no special joints to make and the box is simply glued together.

PREPARATION
Using the ruler and pencil, measure the strip of pine into 2 short rectangles of the same dimension and 2 longer ones. Clamp them onto a work bench and saw them apart.

1 ▲ Glue the pieces of wood together to form a rectangle and then hold them together with masking tape until the glue dries.

2 Place the rectangle on top of a piece of plywood and draw round the inside. Repeat – you need to cut 2 rectangles of plywood. Carefully saw around the lines. Glue the base onto the bottom of the frame, making sure that the base is level with the sides.

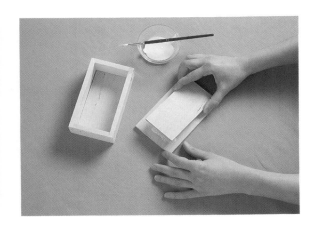

3 ▲ Draw round the outside of the box onto the plywood and cut out this piece to make the

lid. Taking the second of the inside pieces, sand the edges so that the piece fits snugly but easily into the box, round the edges. Spread glue all over the plain side of this and place it centrally on the lid. Turn the lid over and place it on the box, moving it slightly to align it properly.

4 To paint the box, cover with 2 coats of white emulsion (latex) and leave to dry. Paint the base and lid with green acrylic, using a dabbing motion or a sponge to give a textured effect.

5 ▲ Use small, even dabs of white and yellow paint to give a pointillist effect of flowers.

6 Trace a sheep onto plywood by transferring the outline. If you plan to make other animals, keep the shapes as simple as possible for ease of sawing. Use the coping saw to cut round the shapes. Add as many sheep as you like – 3 look well balanced. ▶

Materials and equipment

- *ruler*
- *pencil*
- *strip of pine, about 1cm (½in) thick*
- *G-clamp*
- *work bench*
- *fine-bladed saw*
- *PVA (white) glue*
- *masking tape*
- *plywood*
- *sandpaper*
- *white emulsion (latex) paint*
- *paintbrushes*
- *acrylic paints*
- *coping saw*

7 ◀ Sand the sheep and paint with 2 coats of white emulsion. Leave to dry, then paint creamy-white, with details in brown and black acrylic.

Crackle-varnish salt box

A crackle or ageing effect can be created on any wooden box by applying two different kinds of varnish, one on top of the other. One varnish should be water-based and the other solvent-based. As the second varnish dries it crackles. To increase the effect of the crackle, burnt umber or sienna oil paint can be rubbed into the cracks.

DESIGNING A CRACKLE-VARNISH BOX

Choose a simple or folk design in keeping with this technique. Early American folk art designs in bright bold colours and simple motifs look particularly good.

1 ▲ Paint the box with the base colour and allow to dry. Plan your chosen design on a piece of paper. Transfer to the box by placing a piece of carbon paper face down on the box, and tracing over the drawing.

LEFT: Crackle-varnish salt box by Katie Scampton. Salt boxes were traditionally hung by the fireside to preserve the precious commodity within. This one has been painted with a simple motif and then treated with two varnishes with different drying times. The result is a crackle or crazed look on the surface of the box.

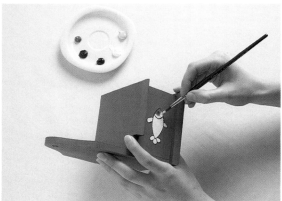

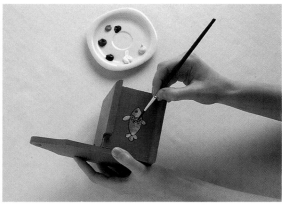

2 ▲ Paint your design over the pencil lines. For best results, dilute the paint and cover the design with a thin wash to begin with, then add depth of colour as you work.

3 ▲ Add more details and depth of colour to the design. ▶

Materials and equipment

- *wooden salt box*
- *acrylic paints or oils (allow for extra drying time if using oils)*
- *paintbrushes*
- *pencil*
- *paper*
- *carbon paper*
- *patina-varnish*
- *2 wide natural hair paintbrushes to apply the varnish*
- *crackle-varnish*
- *burnt umber or sienna oil paint (optional)*
- *soft, lint-free cloth (optional)*

4 Allow the paint to dry, which in the case of acrylic will only take 2–3 minutes. Paint the patina-varnish on the box with a wide natural hair paintbrush. Leave for 12 hours and then apply another layer of varnish. Wait for this to become just dry to the touch. How long this takes will greatly depend on the temperature of the room. You can speed it up by placing the box by a warm radiator but take care: if the radiator is too hot, the wood will warp.

5 When the second layer of varnish is dry to the touch, apply an even layer of crackle-varnish with a different brush. Again, depending on the temperature of the room, the crackles should appear after about 15–20 minutes. If the varnish does not crackle the room is too cold. If this is the case, wash off the last layer of varnish with water and start again.

6 ▲ If you wish to give an 'aged' look to the piece, once the varnish is dry, rub burnt umber or sienna oil paint into the cracks, using a soft cloth. When the colour is dry, apply another layer of patina-varnish to the whole box to give it a protective coat.

Naive-style box

Painted surface design is nothing new: in the United States, it was the primary form of decoration during the eighteenth and nineteenth centuries. Paint was popular for two reasons – the first was that it was inexpensive, the second that paint was an easy way to express local fashions and traditional cultural identities. Free-hand painting can elevate a mundane object from the commonplace to the exceptional. The imagery chosen to decorate this box is naive in character and is similar to images found on pieces of Pennsylvania Dutch folk art.

The animals are based on a Shaker ABC book, although the Shakers did not decorate their boxes, whereas by the nineteenth century the Pennsylvania Dutch were enthusiastically decorating their furniture, walls and textiles. Boxes from this time can be seen at the Metropolitan Museum of Art and the Museum of American Folk Art in New York and the American Museum in Bath, England. Examples include decorated bentwood trinket boxes, candle boxes, and painted or carved wood salt boxes. One of the most popular kinds of box dating from this

LEFT: Naive-style box by Katie Scampton. Inspired by the Shaker ABC book, this toy chest has been painted with acrylics onto natural-coloured wood. A simple border design has been made with the aid of strips of masking tape.

time is the blanket box or chest. Different American communities tended to use motifs common to the area although individual blanket boxes were unique. Sometimes they were painted in panels; at other times the design would be all over the box or only on the front and sides.

DESIGNING A NAIVE-STYLE BOX

Either copy the design illustrated in the photograph or look at the folk art sections in museums of decorative art for inspiration. The imagery does not have to be on a box; it could come from an illustrated book, a piece of china or fabric, knitting, tapestry, or wallpaper. Numerous im-

ages can be adapted, and as the aim is for a 'naive' style, it does not require professional drawing skills.

PREPARATION

Because the effect you are trying to achieve is a naive folk art box, the preparation can be minimal. There is no need to fill in cracks or smooth down the surface – any blemishes will add to the charm of the piece.

Make sure the surfaces are clean and non-greasy by washing down well with detergent and water. If you want to give the box a uniform background colour, use an emulsion which will give a flat colour on which to put your design.

Materials and equipment

- *wooden box*
- *ruler*
- *paper*
- *pencil*
- *masking tape*
- *acrylic paints*
- *paintbrushes*
- *craft knife*
- *carbon paper*
- *fibre-tipped pen, if necessary*
- *matt (flat) polyurethane varnish (optional)*
- *flat paintbrush, for varnishing (optional)*

1 Measure each of the sides of the box, and the lid, and draw up a design to fit these dimensions.

2 ▲ To make a patterned border, place strips of masking tape round the edge of the box at even intervals. Either use the masking tape to measure the intervals or measure them with a ruler.

3 ▲ Apply the paint to the gaps between the masking tape. When the paint is dry remove the tape. You can use the same method to mask out an area for the grass, by using a craft knife to cut a ragged edge in the masking tape.

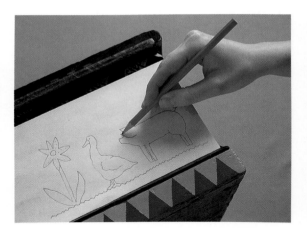

4 ▲ Using masking tape, stick a piece of carbon paper onto one side of the box and then stick the design over it. Using a sharp pencil, trace over the outline of the design. Remove the carbon paper and the paper bearing the design. Repeat the process for the other sides and for the front of the box.

5 ▲ If the pencil lines are very faint go over them with a thicker pencil or a very fine fibre-tipped pen. Using a medium paintbrush, fill in the larger flat areas of the design .

6 ◄ Using a finer paintbrush, add details such as features, fur or any fine lines. You may find your painting needs to be outlined in some areas for it to be properly interpreted.

7 If you wish, use a wide, flat paintbrush to apply a matt varnish over the painted areas of the box, or over the whole box, as a layer of protection.

Stencilled box

Stencilling has been successfully used to decorate everything from manuscripts, furniture, walls and floors for hundreds of years. Paper patterns, dating from the tenth century, which have been pierced with holes and stained with red earth paint, provide evidence of the earliest stencils. These were used to repeat the outline of Buddha numerous times in the Caves of a Thousand Buddhas in Western China.

It was not until the fifteenth century that stencils became popular in Europe, when they were used to overlay colour onto playing cards and wallpaper. During the eighteenth century, American Colonists also used stencils as a cheap alternative to hand-blocked wallpaper. For their inspiration they turned to natural forms such as fruit, trees and eagles.

Traditionally, stencils were cut from heavy paper stiffened in oil or shellac. Designs were created with a number of single stencils, each with a separate motif. Paint was applied with a brush and metallic powders were rubbed into the surface with the fingertips or a velvet pad.

After about 1815, stencilling became one of the most popular methods of decorating. Bronze powder was most commonly applied but other metallic powders including silver, brass, zinc and gold were also used. Large workshops and factories were set up at this time and with this came the standardization of design and motifs.

DESIGNING STENCILS

To translate a design into one that may be stencilled, you need to simplify it and adapt the shapes so that they can have 'bridges'. Bridges are small spaces between parts of the design, which help hold the design together. They give a characteristic look to stencils and give strength

*RIGHT: Stencil box by
Katie Scampton. Stencils
can be ready-cut or you
can make and design
your own. Stencils need
bridges to hold the
different parts of the
design together. These
occur naturally in this
design in the stripes of
the bee and the hive.*

to the material from which you are cutting the
design. Sometimes several bridges are needed for
one part of the design, to stop it moving when
you print and to prevent paint seeping underneath the stencil.

CHOICES OF MATERIALS FOR STENCILLING

There is such a wide choice of materials available
for stencilling that it is sometimes difficult to
know where to start.

Stencil card is a brown, flexible, oiled cardboard which is very easy to cut but which is
opaque. This means the design can be transferred directly onto it but you cannot see through it
when printing. Plastic transparent film is a more
modern material used for stencilling and it lasts
longer than stencil card. It is easy for registering

a design because you can see through it, so it is
ideal when you wish to print two or three
colours.

When stencilling, always apply the palest
colour first. Stencil crayons are wax-based, are
very easy to use and give a soft finish. Quick-
drying stencil paints are sold in specialist shops.
You may also use acrylics, household emulsion,
and cellulose car paints.

APPLYING PAINT

Stencil paint is applied fairly dry, which helps
prevent paint from spreading underneath the
stencil onto other areas of the design. It also
means you can build up colour or keep it only as
a faint suggestion. Use a flat brush. Dip the ends
of the brush into the paint and then dab off any
excess onto absorbent paper.

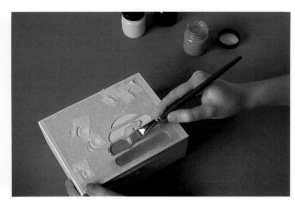

Materials and equipment

- *stencil film or card*
- *masking tape*
- *a rubberized cutting mat, cutting board or a thick piece of card*
- *craft knife*
- *pencil*
- *wooden box*
- *stencil paints*
- *paintbrushes*
- *absorbent paper*

1 ▲ Tape the design onto the cutting mat and tape the film over it. Cut through the film. Alternatively, trace the design onto stencil card and cut. When cutting out a stencil, always cut towards you, and turn the stencil rather than the craft knife.

2 ▲ Tape the stencil onto the box lid and hold it tight with one hand while applying the paint with the other. Lift off the design and leave the paint to dry before applying paint to the side of the box.

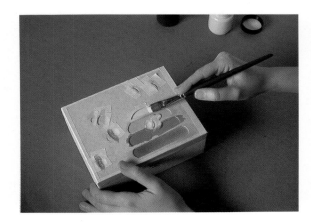

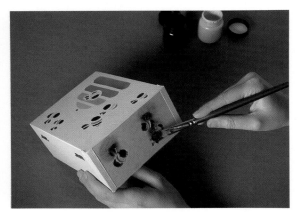

3 ▲ Paint the other three sides of the box in turn, allowing each side to dry before painting the next. If you are using more than one stencil, stick the next stencil over the top of the box. Make sure that it registers with the design already painted.

4 ▲ Apply the paint. Leave it to dry and then repeat the process with the other sides. Continue in this way until the stencilling is complete.

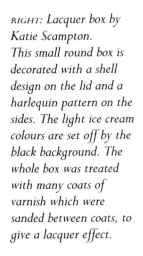

RIGHT: Lacquer box by Katie Scampton.
This small round box is decorated with a shell design on the lid and a harlequin pattern on the sides. The light ice cream colours are set off by the black background. The whole box was treated with many coats of varnish which were sanded between coats, to give a lacquer effect.

Lacquer box

Painting a box black or maroon and then applying many coats of varnish can give the illusion of fine lacquer work. Lacquer ware was particularly popular in England during the seventeenth and eighteenth centuries when a whole papier mâché industry grew up around a popular design style. Early English lacquer work was usually black and often inlaid with mother-of-pearl. Many of these early papier mâché artefacts were boxes, often used to hold luxury items such as tea or playing cards.

PREPARATION

As with all the projects in this book, you can either decorate the complete box or just part of it. You could look at traditional Japanese influences for your motifs, perhaps a design from a woodcut. Alternatively, rather than painting a design you could use pearlized sequins to give a mother-of-pearl inlaid appearance to your box.

Materials and equipment

- *wooden box*
- *pencil*
- *acrylic paints, of various colours, including black*
- *medium and fine paintbrushes*
- *patina-varnish*
- *wide brush for varnish*
- *turpentine*
- *fine sandpaper*

1 ▲ With the pencil draw the design onto the box. This design includes a shell motif on the lid, and a triangular pattern around the sides. If you are not confident about drawing freehand, the design may be transferred onto the box with carbon paper.

2 ▲ Using the pencil marks as a guide, paint the outline of your design using a very fine brush. Here, the triangles on the sides were outlined and filled in with pale, ice cream shades of orange, yellow, pink and green.

3 ▲ Paint the lid by outlining the shell motif in pale pink, and filling in the main shape. Leave to dry. Using a fine paintbrush, paint in the details, such as the ribs on the shell and the border motif.

4 ▲ Pour the black paint into a saucer and mix with a little water. The paint needs to be an even consistency which will flow onto the box. Using a medium brush, paint the background of the box. Start with the lid and be careful not to go over your painted design. ▶

5 When the lid is dry, turn the box on its side and paint the rest of the background. Open the box and paint the inside.

Wash the brush in water immediately after you finish as acrylic paints are impervious to water once dry.

6 When all the sides are dry, apply the patina-varnish to the top of the box using a soft wide brush; this will allow for an even coverage. Try to put the varnish on in a thin rather than a thick layer, as this is less likely to leave streak marks.

Wash the varnish brush in turpentine after use and between each coat.

7 Sand the box between coats. This will make it look dull but this is only temporary; the gloss will re-appear with the next coat of varnish. Apply 3 coats of varnish.

Gilded box

Materials and equipment

- *wooden box*
- *ready-made gesso in white, red or ochre*
- *paintbrush*
- *face mask*
- *silicone carbide paper*
- *wire wool*
- *bole (optional)*
- *soft cloth or cotton wool (batting)*
- *pencil*
- *gold size*
- *Dutch gold transfer leaf*

Gold, always a symbol of status and wealth, has a magical and seductive quality. Because it is so expensive, when it is used for gilding it is beaten into wafer thin layers. Today, it is possible to gild with Dutch gold which looks just as good.

DESIGNING A GILDED BOX

There are various considerations to be taken into account when designing a gilded box. Do you want the gilding to cover all of the box or only part of it? Will you cover the whole box in gesso and then colour it before gilding? Or do you only want to apply gesso to certain areas, using it as a modelling material? A small box will probably look better covered in gold leaf than a large box, which might look too ostentatious. Another design idea is to cut the gold leaf into shapes and apply them as a solid pattern.

PREPARATION

Gesso dust can cause an asthmatic attack, so wear a face mask when sanding. Wash your hands or the gold leaf may stick to them.

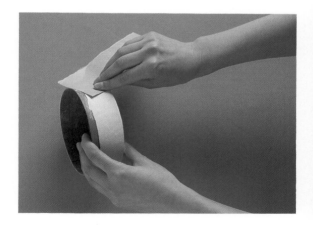

1 ▲ Paint on the gesso in 3–4 layers. Sand the last layer with silicone carbide paper and then wire wool. When the gesso is smooth the box is ready to be coloured or gilded. ▶

LEFT: Gilded box by Katie Scampton. These boxes were covered in gesso (rabbit size and plaster of Paris), then painted, gilded and varnished. Gilding is a long process, but worth it for the beautiful result.

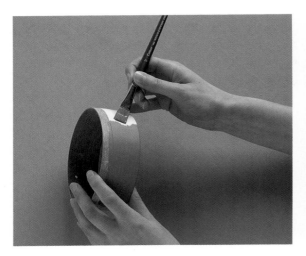

2 ▲ If you wish to colour white gesso, rub bole into the surface with a soft cloth, or apply paint with a paintbrush.

4 ▲ When the gold size is almost dry but still tacky, press a sheet of Dutch gold over the design and peel away the waxed backing paper. The edges will look ragged.

5 After the gold leaf has dried on the design, with a soft cloth or cotton wool (batting), gently rub away the loose leaf which remains.

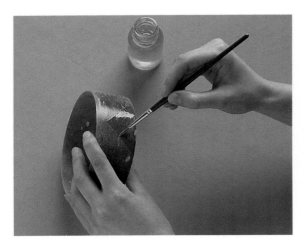

6 If you want an unoxidized, clean bright finish, brush gold size over the design a few days after it has set. For a distressed look, rub over the design with wire wool. The bole will then show through from underneath the gold leaf.

3 ▲ Draw the outline of your design onto the box. Paint the gold size over the design.

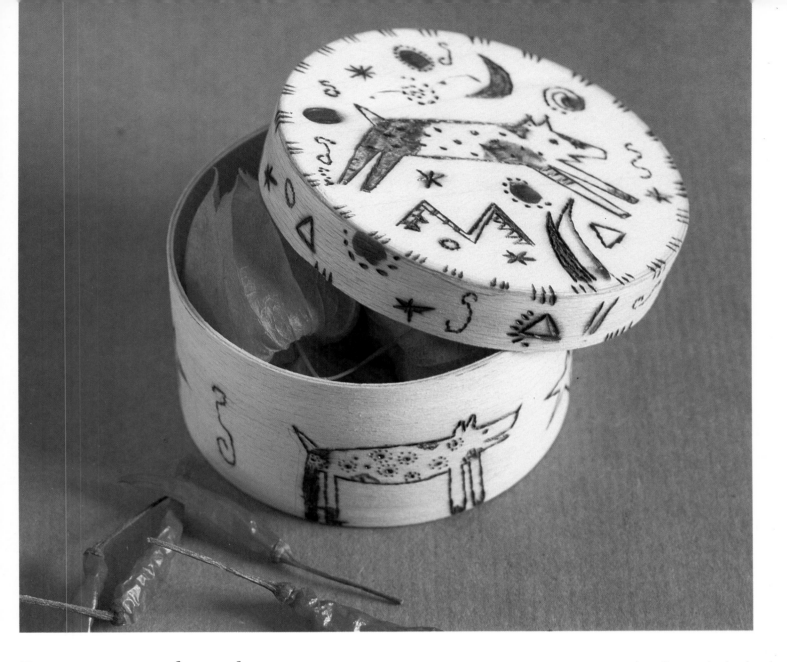

Pyrographic box

Pyrography is the name given to the ancient technique of burning patterns into wood or leather with a heated metal implement. The word is Greek in origin, meaning fire and writing.

The art of pyrography dates back centuries but seems to have originated as a folk art in northern Europe. During the nineteenth century, interest in pyrographic design flourished when the Victorians took to this craft.

Today pyrography is usually practised using a

ABOVE : *Pyrographic box by Katie Scampton. In the hands of a competent practitioner a pyrographic machine can produce wonderful results, such as the little box here with its naive-style patterns.*

ABOVE: A set of boxes decorated with pyrography, or poker work. The two on the left are tobacco boxes, the two on the right are Russian in origin and are made for export to the West.

temperature of the working point cannot be adjusted by the user. As it is by controlling the temperature that the depth of burning – and therefore the colour – is controlled, the artist is partly at the mercy of the instrument.

The hot wire tool has a nib, instead of a solid working point, which is made from a short length of nickel chromium wire, bent into a wishbone shape and held between two terminals at the end of the holder. This tool is excellent for fine line drawing, but a fair amount of skill is necessary for successful results.

The external element pyrograph was used for this box. It incorporates solid working points, each of which has its own heating element close to the tip. The points screw into the end of the holder and operate at a low voltage from a controller. With this tool, the operator is able to control the temperature. A good selection of points of different sizes and shapes makes this a most versatile machine for skilled practitioners and equally suitable for beginners.

small electric machine with an attached 'pencil'. The pencil is heated via the machine and this makes it easy to control the temperature.

THE PYROGRAPHIC MACHINE OR TOOL

There are three types of machine you can buy to do pyrography – the soldering iron type, the hot wire tool, and the external element pyrograph.

The first works on the same principle as a soldering iron with the point of the tool being heated by a cylindrical element or coil inside it. The major disadvantage with this tool is that the

PREPARATION

Use a soft pencil to draw your design onto the box, or transfer a design using carbon paper. You could also use objects such as lids of jars and caps from tubes to draw round. As long as you use a soft pencil, you should be able to rub out any mistakes with an eraser.

Until you feel completely confident using a pyrographic tool, keep the design fairly simple. Remember that the tool should not be used like a pen or pencil.

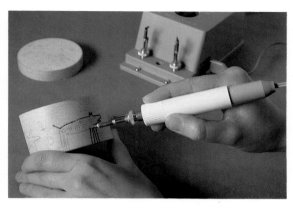

Materials and equipment

- *wooden box*
- *medium- and fine-grade sandpaper*
- *pencil*
- *carbon paper*
- *pyrographic machine*

1 ▲ Using medium and then fine-grade sandpaper, smooth down the outsides of the box. Using a pencil, draw or trace the design straight onto the wood.

2 ▲ Work the design carefully with the tool set at a low temperature at first. Burn in the outline with a fine tip.

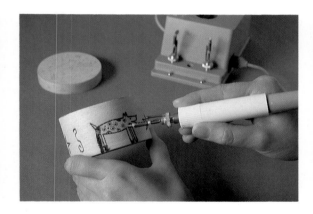

3 ▲ Add detail and shading with a flat or a spoon-shaped tip. Keep the dial at a constant low temperature.

4 ▲ To add darker shadows, raise the temperature of the tool. The hotter the tool, the darker the marks made will be.

Metal Boxes

This section includes two ideas for metal boxes inspired by folk art techniques and designs. One of the boxes started life as a simple wooden cigar box, and was decorated with beaten panels of punched tin which were originally tin cans! The other box is painted in a popular folk style known as canal ware, incorporating loose, fluid brush-strokes in vibrant colours. The effect is achieved quite quickly once you've familiarized yourself with the technique.

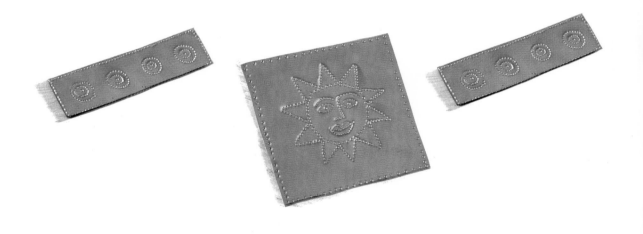

Punched tin box

Tin ware has been – and still is – produced as a form of folk craft in many countries throughout the world. Punched tin ware seems to have been developed in the United States by the Pennsylvania Dutch in the nineteenth century, although pieces are also known to have existed in Victorian England.

The tin ware of the Pennsylvania Dutch was not in fact made entirely of tin, but of sheet iron which was rolled thin, cleaned in a pickling solution, and then dipped in molten tin. The thin tin coating protected the iron from rust. This method of producing tin, which was known as charcoal tin, originated in England, from where it was exported across the Atlantic.

It is thought that originally punched tin ware was made mainly by tinkers although plumbers, who have easy access to the raw materials

required, are known to have turned their hands to the craft in their spare time.

The traditional method of punching tin ware was as follows. First, the pieces were cut to shape, and then a pattern was embossed on the inside by softly striking a punch to form a depression. Holes were not made unless they were needed for a practical reason – to let heat or light escape, for example. Punched tin was often used instead of glass for the doors of cupboards.

An appealing aspect of working with punched

ABOVE: Tin box by Marion Elliot. This box uses a technique which has its origins in American folk art.

Materials and equipment

- *wooden box*
- *ruler*
- *paper*
- *pencil*
- *old tin cans*
- *scissors or tin snips*
- *protective gloves*
- *indelible pen*
- *nail or a centre punch*
- *tack hammer*
- *panel pins (tacks)*
- *cutting board*

tin is that you can recycle old tin cans. They cut well with tin snips or scissors and are easy to work and manipulate. Easier still is metal foil which you can buy in strip form from sculpture suppliers. It comes in copper and brass, giving a pleasing variety of colours.

You can punch your design directly onto a metal box such as a tobacco tin, or you can punch onto pieces of tin and then tack these or bend them round a wooden box. Some designs lend themselves well to punched tin ware, particularly simple patterns such as hearts, spirals, circles and other geometric shapes. Japanese punched stencil designs are another source of inspiration worth investigating. American appliqué quilts with their stylized birds and leaves are a good source for motifs, especially the tulip which is universal in folk art.

PREPARATION

If you are using a tin box with a design on it, remove this with a paint stripper before you begin. Do not use wire wool because this will scratch the tin.

Practise on a spare piece of tin before you start your project. This will help you get a feel for how hard you need to punch in order to achieve an even design. Punching needs to be done with a light touch. To achieve different sized bumps and nodules and holes, vary the size of the nail.

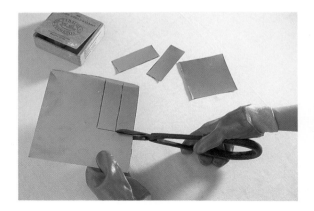

1 ▲ Measure the wooden box and draw a design which will fit onto it. Wearing the protective gloves, cut the tin to the dimensions of the design, with a piece for the lid and for each of the 4 sides.

2 ▲ Place the tin with the wrong side facing upwards, and draw on the design with an indelible pen.

3 ▲ Place the tin on the board and then position the nail on the pen line and punch with the hammer. Move the nail along the line and punch again. Continue until all the design has been punched, then turn the tin round the correct way.

4 ▲ Using short panel pins, hammer the metal panels onto the wooden box.

Canal boat-style metal box

Although the inspiration for this metal box comes from the style of narrow-boat painting popularized by waterway travellers of England, painted tin ware is also popular in China and among the Slavonic nations of eastern Europe. Narrow-boat painting was traditionally applied to three basic utensils: the Buckby can – a covered watering can used to hold drinking water; a hand bowl which was used for scooping canal water for washing; and a nosh bowl from which the canal horse ate its oats.

Choosing to decorate this biscuit tin is in keeping with the narrow-boat dwellers' habit of decorating utilitarian objects. The traditional colours for narrow-boat painting – black, green, red and yellow – were chosen because they were the cheapest to buy and were readily available.

DESIGNING THE BOX

The style of narrow-boat painting is often known as 'castles and roses' as these are the most popular images used. Roses were painted because they appeared so regularly along the canal towpaths. The castles are thought to resemble those buildings found in the Carpathian Mountains of eastern Europe.

RIGHT: Canal-style painted box by Katie Scampton, with the design known as 'castles and roses'. In the background are brightly-painted Russian folk art boxes made of wood.

The key to successful narrow-boat painting is to take your time. Concentrate on building up the design in layers, starting with the background colour, moving onto the base colour for the leaves and roses and then finally adding the decorative detail.

PREPARATION

It is a good idea to practise on an old piece of metal to get the feel of the loose brush stroke. Ceramic, enamel or cellulose paints can all be used to give a shiny finish, but be careful not to mix different types of paint together.

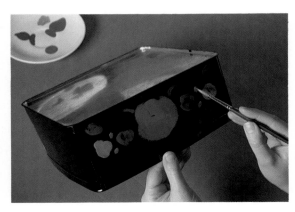

Materials and equipment

- *metal box*
- *medium- and fine-grade sandpaper*
- *a selection of paint suitable for painting on metal*
- *fine and medium paintbrushes*
- *wide natural hair paintbrush, for varnishing*
- *turpentine, for cleaning brushes*
- *clear varnish*

1 ▲ Sand down the box until it is smooth, and clean away the dust. Paint the background black with a thick paintbrush. When dry, sand with fine sandpaper.

2 ▲ Paint the background forms of the design for the roses and the leaves in freehand. Leave to dry between stages.

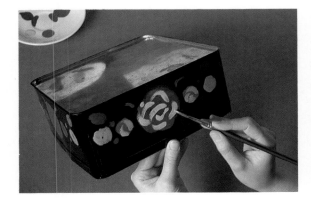

3 ▲ Paint the petals and the leaf markings with single, swift brush strokes using a fine brush.

4 ▲ Add dots and dashes for the flower centres using an even finer brush. Leave to dry. When the paint is completely dry, finish with a coat of clear varnish.

Novelty Boxes

The range of boxes in this section is truly extraordinary and some of the boxes and methods are so unusual they should really be in a class all their own. Included is a box inspired by the Victorian pastime of tinsel painting, resulting in a light-reflecting creation in jewel-bright colours. There is a wonderful shell box – another Victorian update – reminiscent of driftwood and the seaside, as well as a box decorated with mosaic. Finally there is a box constructed entirely of gingerbread, which would make a tempting table decoration filled with candies and gingerbread men. These unique storage ideas may tempt you to develop your own.

TOP: Shell box by Katie Scampton.

ABOVE: Tinsel box by Katie Scampton.

*RIGHT: Mosaic box by Katie Scampton.
A freehand mosaic pattern can be made up from pieces of broken china. Arrange the pieces in an abstract pattern or a simple picture and stick with tile cement and grout as you would tiles.*

Mosaic box

A mosaic is an image or design made from tiny pieces (usually squares, of glass, stone or tile) which are known as tesserae. Mosaics are also made from marble and smooth pebbles. Vitreous glass squares can be bought from mosaic dealers in a standard size of 2cm (¾in).

PREPARATION

Working with mosaic is a fairly messy process because it involves cement, so find a good work area where you will not be disturbed.

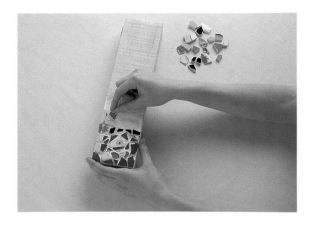

3 ▲ Start by working the perimeters of the main shapes in the design. Stick each piece in place with glue.

Materials and equipment

- *wooden box*
- *pencil*
- *paper or graph paper*
- *eraser*
- *knife*
- *pieces broken china in various colours*
- *PVA (white) glue*
- *tile grouting, or grey sand cement, mixed*
- *palette knife*
- *trowel*
- *rubber gloves*
- *hydrochloric acid and brush*
- *cloths and sponges*
- *wax furniture polish*

1 ▲ Draw the design for the lid, the sides, the front and the back of the box onto paper and decide which colours you plan to use.

2 Transfer the design freehand onto the box. Use a soft pencil so that you can rub out any mistakes, and adjust as necessary. When you are pleased with what you have drawn, score the surface of the box with a knife to give a key for the adhesive.

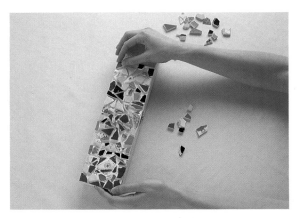

4 ▲ If the design continues from the lid to the box edges, work each part of the pattern ignoring the separation between the lid and box, so that the pattern will flow. ▶

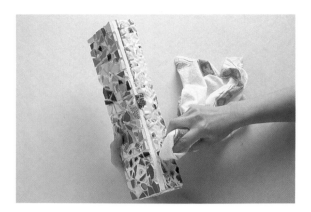

5 ◄ Grout between the pieces of china with grey sand cement and leave to dry for 3–4 days. Wear rubber gloves for protection and clean the surface of the design with hydrochloric acid. The acid will help to prevent a grey appearance where some of the mosaic may pick up cement dust. When it is dry, polish the box with a wax furniture polish to bring out the colour.

RIGHT: Mosaic box by Glen Morgan. The use of gold and mirror tiles creates a light-reflecting quality, and textural variety.

LEFT: *Shell box by Katie Scampton. Shell boxes were originally made by sailors away at sea. They then became a popular Victorian hobby. This modern shell box is painted a pale blue-grey like the sea, with a central star motif.*

Shell box

Shell boxes have long been in existence but were particularly popular during the Victorian era when parlour pastimes were in their heyday. This was due to the abundance of cheap, domestic labour which gave the majority of upper and middle-class young women time in which they could carry out their favourite hobbies. Two of the most popular activities of the day included modelling wax flowers and making boxes decorated with shells.

Shell work usually took the form of pictures, but sometimes was used for three-dimensional designs, such as dolls or bouquets of flowers, which were presented under glass domes. Shell pictures were not just the preserve of young ladies in the nineteenth century. Shell boxes and pictures – also known as 'sailors' valentines' – were worked by sailors on long voyages for their loved ones at home. These valentine pictures were enclosed in a frame hinged to a box. The frame was enclosed behind glass so that the shells were protected from possible damage. The shells were usually arranged in a formal, intricate pattern and sometimes included a motto worked in shells. Sometimes a heart was included in the centre of the pattern.

Materials and equipment

- *wooden box*
- *assorted shells of different colours and sizes*
- *acrylic paint*
- *paintbrushes*
- *pencil*
- *paper*
- *PVA (white) glue or plaster of Paris*

DESIGNING A SHELL BOX

Plan the design to suit the shape of the box, which could be oval, square, heart-shaped or whatever you choose. You may be able to buy a box with a glass top and false bottom to the lid, so that you can enclose the design within it, or you can stick shells all over a plain box.

PREPARATION

Scrub all the shells with warm soapy water and leave them to dry. Then sort the shells into groups according to colour and size.

1 ▲ Paint the box with your chosen colour. This box was not sanded, to keep a rough appearance reminiscent of driftwood.

2 Depending on the number and size of the shells in your possession, either draw a pattern on paper or arrange the shells on a flat surface beside the box. Use the larger shells to form a central motif and surround this with smaller ones. The prettiest shells might best be displayed with their insides facing outwards.

3 ▲ Starting with the centre of the design, stick the shells onto the box with PVA glue. Gradually work outwards.

4 ▲ Add more detail, filling in more of the design with smaller shells.

5 If you decide to use plaster of Paris remember that it sets quickly. You will have to be more accurate when positioning the shells as they will be difficult to move once the plaster of Paris has begun to solidify.

LEFT: Tinsel box by Katie Scampton. This is a modern version of a typically Victorian craft. The glass or transparent lid of the box is decorated with glass paint. Behind the paint, a piece of tin foil is scrunched, offsetting the luminous colours.

Tinsel box

An unusual way to decorate a glass-lidded box is with tinsel painting – or crystal painting as it is sometimes known – which started in the United States in the early 1850s. Exotic flowers, birds, and other natural forms were painted onto mirror or glass which had a piece of crumpled foil behind it. This enhanced the colours so they appeared to glow. Originally, opaque oil colours were used, but today it is better to work with paints which are made specifically for glass.

DESIGNING FOR TINSEL PAINTING

Painting onto glass is not as easy as painting onto other surfaces, because the paint will not always lie flat. It is best to work in a dust-free atmosphere or you may end up with a fuzzy image. Try to nudge the paint into position rather than use heavy brushwork. A non-repetitive, free design – perhaps floral – is easiest to start with.

Materials and equipment

- *box with glass top, and backing to support the silver foil*
- *silver foil*
- *scissors*
- *paper*
- *pencil*
- *masking tape*
- *paintbrushes*
- *glass paints*
- *turpentine for cleaning glass and brushes*

PREPARATION

Cut a piece of foil 5cm (2in) bigger than the lid of the box.

1 ▲ Draw your design on paper, then cut it out to fit under the glass.

2 ▲ Remove the glass from the top of the box. Tape the paper with the design on it under the glass. Following the design on the paper underneath as a guide paint flat areas with opaque colours.

3 ▲ Build up the design with more colours. Glass and ceramic paints tend to give quite a solid colour. If a lighter colour is required, dilute the paint with turpentine. Rinse out the brushes between colours to prevent them from becoming muddy. Leave the glass in a horizontal position in a dust-free room for about 24 hours while the paint dries.

4 ▲ Gently scrunch the previously cut foil and put it in the lid of the box. The foil will enhance the rich colours of the glass.

LEFT: Gingerbread box by Ann Marie Mulligan. Gingerbread has been used to make boxes and houses in many communities all round the world from the United States to Scandinavia, Germany, Switzerland and Austria. This box has a simple design and is decorated with royal icing.

Gingerbread box

Food is usually stored in a box of one kind or another, but the position may be reversed and the box itself made of food! Boxes can be made from chocolate, fondant icing, or, as in this case, dough. Gingerbread may be decorated with any kind of icing. Traditional white icing looks best against the dark background, but colours could be added in the form of sweets (candies).

Materials and equipment

For the gingerbread
- *700g/2½lb/10 cups plain (all-purpose) flour*
- *2tsp bicarbonate of soda (baking soda)*
- *2tsp salt*
- *2tsp cloves*
- *2tsp nutmeg*
- *4tsp cinnamon*
- *4tsp ginger*
- *500g/1lb/2 cups vegetable shortening*
- *4 eggs, beaten*
- *340g/12oz/2½ cups molasses*
- *500g/1lb/2 cups sugar*

For the royal icing
- *2 egg whites*
- *¼tsp lemon juice*
- *450g/1lb/3 cups icing (confectioners') sugar, sieved (sifted)*
- *1tsp glycerine*

To decorate
- *card (posterboard)*
- *scissors*
- *rolling pin*
- *board*
- *25 × 25cm (10 × 10in) square of cardboard covered in foil*
- *icing bag and nozzles*

PREPARATION

Preheat the oven to 180°C/350°F/Gas Mark 4. In a large bowl mix the flour, bicarbonate of soda (baking soda), salt and spices. In a saucepan, melt the shortening over a gentle heat. Cool until luke-warm, then pour into the bowl of a food processor, and add the flour, eggs, molasses and sugar. Blend on medium until all the ingredients are mixed and have formed a dough.

To make the royal icing, place the egg whites and lemon juice in a bowl, and gradually add the icing sugar, stirring constantly to achieve a smooth consistency. Stir in the glycerine until well blended.

3 ▲ Assemble the 4 sides of the box on the base by piping icing and using it as glue.

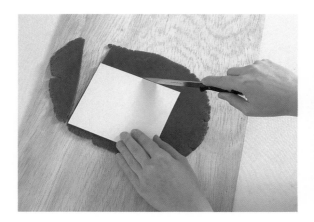

1 ▲ Cut a template of card (posterboard) measuring 13 × 12cm (5¼ × 4¾in). Roll out the gingerbread dough and use the template as a guide to cut out the 4 box sides, the base and the lid.

2 Bake the pieces of gingerbread on a baking sheet for 15–20 minutes until the edges are slightly brown.

4 ▲ Using an icing bag, decorate each side of the box with icing using a simple folk art motif. Make the decoration on the lid more intricate.

LEFT: This wonderful novelty box by Kirsty Rees provides an alternative to a photograph album or scrap book. A three-tier cake box, adorned with fake pearls, candles and candies, is decorated inside with photographs of the designer's past and present.

EMBELLISHING BOXES

Almost any box can be made more interesting with a little embellishment – whether it is made of wood, paper, or fabric-covered. An old box can be revived with ribbons, beads, flowers or jewel-like baubles in next to no time and at very little expense. Gift-giving, too, becomes that much more personal when the container is as delightful as the contents. The following pages illustrate some decorations which can be used as starting points for your own ideas, and highlight ways to create inexpensive yet beautiful presentation boxes to give as gifts.

Decorating Boxes

Many of the projects in this book include ideas for constructing new boxes from unusual materials, but it is a simple matter to decorate an existing box. Often it takes the minimum of time and effort, and the use of ordinary and inexpensive materials, to turn the simplest box into a one-off item.

The following pages should give you plenty of scope to develop your own ideas. There are clever ways with paint and paper; quick and effective methods for applying objects to the outsides of boxes for textural interest, and to the insides of boxes for hidden luxury. There is a treasure chest studded with glass jewels; a charming box with a rabbit-shaped handle; and rich-looking boxes embellished with golden paint effects. You could also consider boxes in printed wallpaper, wrapping paper, or even sheet music. Facsimiles of old maps are often beautiful in their own right, and make wonderful decorative covers for boxes of all sizes. The possibilities are endless.

Petit-fours box

This pretty box started life as a simple wooden cake box. It was painted fire engine red, and studded with inexpensive petit-fours or chocolate moulds. These miniature tin moulds are available from kitchenware shops and department stores.

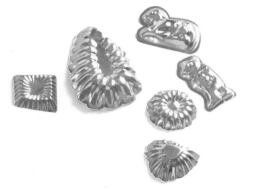

1 ▲ Sand the box to get rid of any rough edges, and wipe down with a cloth. Apply a coat of acrylic paint and allow to dry.

LEFT: Petit-fours box by Marion Elliot. This bright little box would cheer up any kitchen, and could be used to store recipes, tea bags or herbs and spices.

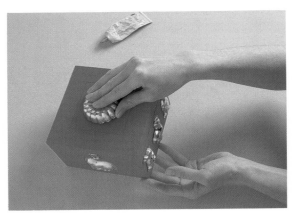

Materials and equipment

- *wooden box*
- *medium-grade sandpaper*
- *acrylic paint*
- *paintbrush*
- *selection of petit-fours or chocolate moulds*
- *strong all-purpose glue*

2 ▲ When you have selected the moulds you plan to use, apply a strong all-purpose glue to the underside of each mould.

3 ▲ Working on one side at a time, stick the mould in position onto the surface of the box, holding for a few seconds to allow the glue to set. Make sure the glue is completely dry on one side before progressing to the next.

RIGHT: Gold-leaf pencil holder by Emma Whitfield. This effect can be used as a quick and luxurious embellishment for many types of box.

Gold-leaf pencil holder

A drab cardboard pencil holder is completely transformed with gold leaf applied to a terracotta-coloured base. The gold leaf is gently rubbed with wire to reveal the base coat underneath, creating a rich depth of colour and textural interest.

1 ▶ Paint the box inside and out with acrylic paint, and leave to dry.

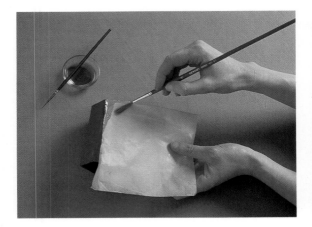

2 ▲ Apply a coating of gold size to the dried surface, and leave to dry until tacky. Using a paintbrush to prevent finger prints, press the gold leaf onto the size.

3 ▲ Leave to dry, then gently rub with a piece of fine wire wool to reveal the paint underneath, giving a distressed look.

Black-work box

Decorate a trinket box or other gift box with acrylic paints and contrasting cut-out paper shapes. A coat of varnish can be added to seal the pieces in place.

1 ▶ Sand the box to get rid of any surface blemishes, and wipe with a damp cloth. Apply a coat of acrylic paint. ▶

RIGHT: Black-work box by Emma Whitfield. Black-work is a form of decoupage which has been practised for centuries. The pattern is made from folded black paper which is glued onto the box.

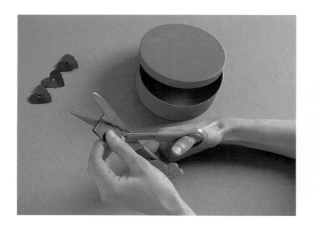

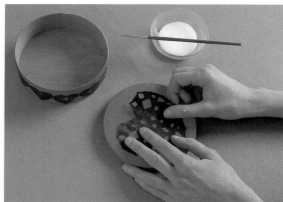

2 ▲ Using ordinary cartridge paper, fold the paper in half and in half again twice. The more the paper is folded the more elaborate the cut-out will be, but make sure the folds are not too thick to cut. Using a small, sharp pair of scissors, such as nail scissors or sewing scissors, cut out small sections of the paper along the folded lines.

3 ▲ Use PVA glue to stick the cut-outs in position, making sure the paper lies absolutely flat, and that the patterns on the sides of the box join accurately. Leave to dry, and seal with a coat of varnish, if desired.

Treasure chest

A small wooden casket is painted and then decorated with small glass studs to create an attractive trinket box.

Materials and equipment

- *wooden box*
- *medium-grade sandpaper*
- *paintbrush*
- *acrylic paint*
- *strong, clear adhesive*
- *glass studs*

2 ▲ Gradually build up the design around each side of the box, holding each stud in position for a few seconds to ensure it sticks to the surface. Allow the studs to dry on each side before working on the next. The pattern may be continued inside the box.

1 ▲ Sand the box to remove any surface blemishes, and wipe with a damp cloth. Paint the outside of the box with acrylic paint, leave to dry, then paint the inside. Leave to dry. Apply strong adhesive to the back of each stud.

RIGHT: Treasure chest by Marion Elliot. The success of this simple box depends on the unusual choice of base colour and brightly-coloured, candy-like glass studs. A more traditional looking treasure chest could be made using gold as the base colour.

Materials and equipment

- *wooden box*
- *medium-grade sandpaper*
- *paintbrushes*
- *acrylic paint*
- *gold paint*
- *wooden ornament*
- *strong, clear adhesive*

Rabbit box

This round wooden box is embellished with a naive-style wooden toy which serves as a handle. Any small toy or object can be added to the lids of boxes for decorative and practical purposes. The box itself may be painted in coordinating or contrasting colours.

Like the other projects in this book, the finished design may be as simple or as ornate as you like.

1 ▲ Sand the box to remove any surface blemishes, and rub down with a damp cloth. Apply a coat of acrylic paint and leave to dry.

2 ▲ Apply a thin layer of gold paint and rub gently with a soft cloth to reveal some of the blue paint underneath. Leave to dry.

LEFT: Rabbit box by Marion Elliot. Small toys or objects in wood or other materials can be used as decorative and functional handles on the lids of boxes.

3 ◀ Stick your chosen ornament to the lid of the box with a strong adhesive.

Presentation Boxes

A presentation box will transform a perhaps quite ordinary gift into something very special. It is almost as if the box becomes part of the present itself.

A gift may be presented in any kind of box – card, metal or wood are likely materials. You can obliterate any advertising in a number of ways depending on how creative and imaginative you want to be. Alternative methods include painting, covering in fabric or glitter, or using decoupage. You could cover the box completely with layers of tissue paper, sweets (candies), stamps or even dried out and varnished biscuits (cookies).

If you are using a wooden box you could line it with a paper doiley, fill it with dried fruit and decorate it with dried rosebuds, raffia and corn. A gift of nuts, for instance, could be arranged in a box covered in moss, acorns and miniature cones. With the simplest ingredients and a little imagination, you can easily make an everyday present look much more special.

BELOW: Christmas box and Forest box by Jan Bridge.

RIGHT: Toiletries box by Jan Bridge. A humble present is made special in sophisticated packaging. A wooden presentation box with a transparent lid is edged with cord. The gifts inside are colour coordinated and tied with ribbons and sprigs of lavender.

Materials and equipment

- *1 glass-topped box*
- *piece of piping cord wide enough to cover the edge of the glass*
- *PVA (white) glue*
- *2 facecloths, 1 white and 1 mauve*
- *narrow mauve ribbon*
- *sprigs of lavender*
- *1 oblong purple bar of soap*
- *tracing paper*
- *narrow white ribbon*
- *2 lengths of tartan ribbon, of different widths*
- *1 round white bar of soap*
- *1 circular loofah*
- *4 purple bath oils*

Toiletries box

A couple of soaps and a fluffy facecloth beautifully wrapped and arranged in a presentation box look much more exciting and expensive than if they were given on their own.

The choice of purple and mauve items in this box reflect the lavender theme, but other items could be included to reflect the taste of the recipient. A blue and white colour scheme could include small decorative shells and a green and yellow scheme could include dried flowers.

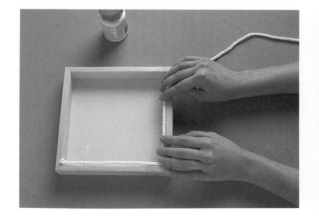

1 ▲ Stick the piping cord round the box lid.

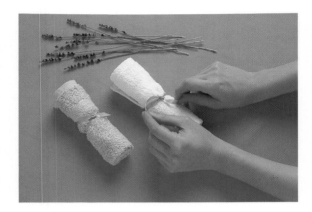

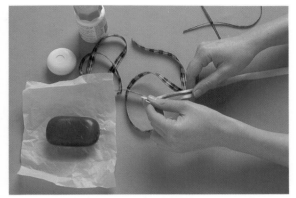

2 ▲ Roll the facecloths into loose sausage shapes and tie with a piece of mauve ribbon. Insert 2 or 3 sprigs of lavender underneath the ribbon.

3 ▲ Wrap the purple oblong soap in a piece of tracing paper. Stick the very narrow tartan ribbon onto the white ribbon with glue. Tie this round the oblong soap. Tie the slightly wider tartan ribbon round the circular soap.

4 Turn the box with the glass side facing the table, and arrange the facecloths, loofah, soaps and bath oils inside. These should fit snugly, so that they stay in position in the box.

BELOW: Dried-flower box by Jan Bridge.

Dried-flower box

This tiny box was decorated with straw-coloured raffia, stalks of wheat and a dried rosebud. The muted colours complement the natural colour of the wood and raffia.

The autumnal feel of the packaging reflects the contents of dried fruits and nuts, creating a mini-harvest to give as a gift. Another seasonal box could be decorated with blue and pink dried flowers such as larkspur (delphinium) and rose-buds, and contain chocolate Easter eggs.

Materials and equipment

- *wooden box*
- *raffia*
- *scissors*
- *stalks of dried wheat*
- *dried rosebuds*
- *dried foliage*

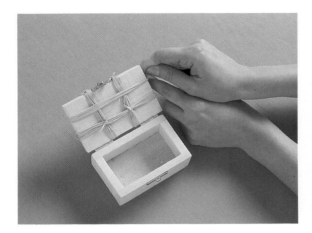

1 ▲ Tie lengths of raffia around the lid, knotting on the underside of the lid. Where the pieces of raffia cross on the top of the lid, knot an extra piece of raffia, and cut the ends short.

2 ▲ The final length of raffia is tied around the lid of the box. On the inside of the lid, knot and cut lengths of raffia as for the top. Slip the stalks of wheat, rosebud and foliage under the raffia.

Materials and equipment

- *paper ribbon (enough to wrap around the box, and tie a generous bow, plus 7.5cm/3in extra)*
- *PVA (white) glue*
- *artificial flowers and foliage*

Paper ribbon presentation box

An elaborate paper bow and artificial flowers and ivy adorn this simple, undecorated box.

Paper ribbon is available from art suppliers and good quality papercraft shops, and comes in a wide variety of colours and patterns. It is sold tightly coiled – you will have to unroll it gently, and smooth it out for a wide, generous bow. Alternatively, you could tie it around the box, still coiled, and unfurl it only at each end.

1 ▲ Unroll the paper ribbon and wrap around the box, parcel fashion. Tie in a half-knot at the top, and form two generous loops.

2 ▲ Wrap the separate piece of ribbon across the centre of the bow, where the two loops join. Apply a strong adhesive to the ends of the separate piece, and secure underneath the loops, forming a false bow.

3 ▲ Finish by inserting small artificial flowers and sprigs of artificial ivy under the ribbon.

ABOVE: Four presentation boxes by Jan Bridge, including a paper ribbon presentation box (top left); a box decorated with dried flowers (bottom left); a wooden box filled with herbs and spices presented in brown paper parcels, with a sequin-decorated lid (top right); and a small wooden box decorated with nuts and artificial moss (bottom right).

Christmas box

This wonderful Christmas box is very simple to make, yet is beautifully effective. It can be adapted for other seasons – adorned with spring flowers for a birthday or Christening, or decorated with dried flowers in the autumn. The only problem will be finding a gift worthy of such a delightful container!

PREPARATION

An oval Shaker-style box was used for the base, but any box of any material may be used. If necessary, the box may be painted or covered in paper. Leave to dry, then glue a block of florist's dry foam to the lid using PVA (white) glue.

Materials and equipment

- *oval, Shaker-style box*
- *paintbrushes (optional)*
- *acrylic paints (optional)*
- *florist's dry foam*
- *PVA (white) glue*
- *cuttings of evergreens such as holly and ivy*
- *wide satin ribbon*

1 ▲ Insert branches of holly and evergreen into the foam. You may choose to work on one side of the foam, matching the other side to the first half, or you may prefer to insert larger cuttings around the perimeter of the foam, and build up the design by filling in the gaps with smaller cuttings and foliage.

2 ▲ When you have achieved a pleasing result, tie a wide ribbon around the box, and finish with a large bow. Adjust the bow so that it sits well on the greenery.

LEFT: *Christmas parcel by Jan Bridge. An oval Shaker-style box was covered in ochre paper and embellished with bands of metallic ribbon and gold and red tinsel. Red baubles and glittery apples were heaped onto the lid, and stuck in place with a strong adhesive.*

RIGHT: Decoupage presentation box by Emma Whitfield.

Decoupage presentation box

A glass-lidded box is given an oriental flavour with the addition of a paper flower cut from wrapping paper and a gold leaf base. It could be used as a container for a gift, or would make a delightful present on its own. Experiment with different paper motifs and colours.

Materials and equipment

- *glass-topped box*
- *masking tape*
- *paintbrushes*
- *acrylic paint*
- *fine scissors*
- *wrapping paper or paper scraps*
- *PVA (white) glue*
- *gold size*
- *Dutch gold transfer leaf*

1 ▲ Line the edge of the glass with masking tape to prevent paint splashing onto the surface, and coat the sides of the box with acrylic paint. When the paint is absolutely dry, carefully remove the masking tape.

2 ▲ Using a pair of very fine scissors, cut out your chosen motif.

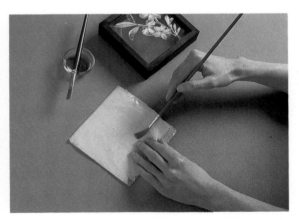

3 ▲ Apply a thin layer of PVA glue to the back of the motif using a fine paintbrush, ensuring that the surface is evenly covered. Position the motif on the glass, making sure the paper lies flat. Remove any air bubbles by carefully rolling the handle of a paintbrush across the paper.

4 ▲ Apply gold size to the cardboard base of the box and leave until tacky. Using a paintbrush, apply the gold leaf and leave to dry. Reposition the base of the box.

THE CARE AND PRESERVATION OF BOXES

Boxes can often be found in a better state than other collectors' items, frequently for a reasonable price. Although some boxes would be best repaired by a professional restorer, there are still many old boxes which you can restore yourself.

Since a box can be made from almost anything, many boxes will inevitably incorporate a variety of materials. You may find that some parts of a box can be cleaned or polished – wood, for example – while other parts, especially if they are made of material such as velvet or silk, may not be cleaned without taking the box to pieces.

Papier mâché

The most effective way to clean papier mâché is to use a cream furniture polish very sparingly on it. Rub this in with a soft cloth, then immediately wipe away the polish with another cloth. This seems to restore the lustre of the papier mâché without harming the printing or inlay decoration. For very dirty areas, soak a soft cloth in soapy water (not detergent), wring it out and gently rub the offending area. Dry with another cloth straightaway. Do not apply pressure to hand-painted areas. Unless you are an expert at painting, do not attempt to paint over areas. Apart from the fact that you may ruin the box, you will definitely detract from any commercial value. Where small chips of the lacquer have fallen off, these may be touched up with indian ink. If you are good with your hands, you could build up the areas which have fallen away with papier mâché before applying the ink. Remember to leave the glue and paste to dry between layers. (Note that papier mâché made with PVA (white) glue is stronger than that made from wallpaper paste.) If your box includes an inlay of mother-of-pearl and it has become loose, you should be able to glue it back. Use glue sparingly and wipe away any excess immediately.

OPPOSITE: Boxes from Kashmir. Papier mâché has been manufactured and exported all over the world from this region for well over a century.

Metal

Brass, pewter, tin and silver can all be cleaned with metal polish but take great care as these polishes are abrasive. Filigree work will lose its patina if it is rubbed too vigorously. When polishing locks or hinges on boxes that are made of other materials, such as wood, make sure that no metal polish touches the wood. If any does wipe it off immediately. Good commercial preparations are available for cleaning metals but do use them with caution. Before you start cleaning a metal box, decide just how new you want it to look. It takes many years for a box to acquire a patina, and this is often more attractive than a shiny new-looking surface.

Enamel boxes can be cleaned with cotton wool (batting) dipped in mild soap and water so long as the box is dried directly after cleaning. Do not try to clean any cracked or bent areas.

OPPOSITE BELOW: Inlaid boxes, clockwise from top – Chinese box with photograph on the lid; mother-of-pearl papier mâché box; dressing table box with inlaid pattern; two small trinket boxes; mosaic cigarette box; Tunbridge ware look-alike calling card case; cigar box with mother-of-pearl inlay.

RIGHT: Contemporary pewter-covered boxes set with central stones and embossed with patterns, by Linda McVicar.

Ivory, shell and mother-of-pearl

Apart from washing, there is very little you can do to clean these natural materials. Ivory and mother-of-pearl should be cleaned in a mild detergent and water solution using cotton wool (batting) balls which have been wrung out. Dry the items immediately with a soft cotton cloth. Do not clean yellowed ivory at all. Tortoiseshell should be cleaned with a mild soap and water solution. For shells, clean out the individual shells with an artist's brush before cleaning with soap and water.

LEFT: Clean shells with a soft, dry paintbrush before wiping with water and a mild soap solution.

Wood

What used to be described as elbow grease – that is, vigorous polishing with cream furniture polish or wax – is probably the best way to restore the patina on a neglected wooden box.

Veneered wood boxes are more difficult to repair. It is very difficult to match wood grains and re-glue loosened veneer, so this is a job best left to experts. A veneered box should always be polished with the grain of the wood. Water should never be used because it will loosen the fish glue with which the veneer has been stuck to the main body of the box.

Inlay

A white wood glue is indispensable when mending boxes, and it is particularly good for replacing inlays of mother-of-pearl, wood or bone. Before re-sticking, use a razor blade to clean out the old glue from the recess and from the back of the piece to be re-stuck. Apply the glue to the

inlay, press the offending piece into place and wipe away any excess glue. If the inlay is from a flat surface, place a weight upon it until it is dry.

Linings

Sometimes the interior of a box will have suffered more wear and tear than its exterior. A box can be re-lined with either fabric or paper. Old fabrics are not easy to come by but they can occasionally be found in thrift shops or at auctions. If you cannot find a suitable fabric, you could use a reproduction modern fabric or alternatively age a fabric by dyeing it in cold tea.

To line a box you will need to cut panels of card slightly smaller than the box they are intended to fit. Glue the fabric to the card, leave to dry and then fit the panels into the box.

Hinges

It is worth collecting old and battered boxes just for their fittings, hinges, handles and locks which may all be re-used on other boxes. A common problem with old boxes is that the hinges sometimes pull away. The easiest way to mend these is to fill the area from which the hinge has come loose with plastic wood. Press the hinge into the plastic wood while the lid is closed. Bind the box with string or masking tape to hold the hinge in place while the plastic wood dries. Then fix the hinge firmly in position with new screws or nails, depending on the type of original fixing.

A lock which has become damaged may be replaced with a lock of the same size. You may be able to find one of a similar vintage from another box.

Buying and collecting boxes

Boxes do not fit neatly into a traditional antiques category, such as clocks, furniture or textiles, so it can be difficult to find out information about them. However, since boxes are made out of so many different materials, the sources for innovative and interesting examples are more abundant than for other artefacts.

Boxes also have the advantage of dating from so many art movements and periods of history. You could choose to collect boxes from a particular period or to collect boxes all made from the same material.

Perhaps advertising fascinates you, in which case you could collect tins. Or you might decide to collect a box designed for a specific purpose – money, snuff or musical boxes, for example. Of course, you do not have to collect old boxes; the boxes of today will become the antiques of tomorrow. You might want to start a collection of boxes in which tea comes, or else choose chocolate or cigarette boxes. The possibilities are endless and your collection does not have to be expensive. Simply follow your own preferences, and keep an eye out for bargains and sources.

LEFT: Decoupage hat boxes by Emma Whitfield. Many artists working today create unique and reasonably priced pieces.

RIGHT: Twentieth-century utility boxes, including a modern turned hardwood string box with a hole in the lid for easy use; a candle box with a brass hinged lid; an early twentieth-century dressing table manicure set and a miniature set of dominoes. Many twentieth-century boxes can still be purchased at reasonable prices, and just might become the collector's items of tomorrow.

FAR RIGHT: Appliquéd chocolate box covered in black velvet and decorated with flowers in shades of pink, with green leaves. Date unknown but believed to be 1920s.

RIGHT AND FAR RIGHT: A typical Victorian **trompe-loeil** *box. Three real books have been stuck together and the insides have been carved out to hold drink and glasses. Victorian boxes are highly sought-after for their skilful workmanship.*

For specialist boxes, the best plan is to visit auction houses which deal in the period in which you are interested. Bric-à-brac, thrift and charity shops can also be good sources of boxes, along with car boot sales. Once people know you collect a certain type of box, they will probably look out for them on your behalf and you can always ask for them as birthday or Christmas presents. As with buying anything, it is a good idea to look around and get a feel of the market before you buy. When you first start your collection, it is best to buy items because you like them and not because you hope they will be a good investment, though with luck they might.

STOCKISTS

ART SUPPLIES

Dylon International Ltd
Worsley Bridge Road
London SE26
UK
(fabric dyes)

Paperchase
213 Tottenham Court Road
London W1 4US
UK

Papersource Inc
730 N Franklin Suite 111
Chicago
Illinois, 60610
USA

ACT Papers Pty Ltd
10 McGlone Street
Micham
Victoria 3132
Australia

E & F Good
31 Landsdowne Terrace
Walkerville   SA 5081
Australia

CERAMIC AND GLASS PAINT SUPPLIES

Art Graphique
Unit 2 Poulton Close
Dover
Kent CT17 0HL
UK

Reeves Art Shop
178 Kensington High Street
London W8 7RG
UK

Duncan Ceramics
5673 East Shields
Fresno
California 93727
USA

DECOUPAGE SUPPLIES

The Dover Bookshop
18 Earlham Street
London WC2 9LN
UK

Hawkin & Co
Saint Margaret
Harleston
Norfolk IP20 0PJ
UK

Dover Publications Inc
31 East 2nd Street
Mineola
New York 11501
USA

Paper E Clips
20 Maud Street
Suite 307
Toronto
Ontario M5Y 2M5
Canada

Rosehain, Lipmann &
Peers Pty Ltd
147 Burnley Street
Richmond
Victoria 3121
Australia

FABRIC AND SEWING SUPPLIES

Borovicks
16 Berwick Street
London W1V 4HP
UK

DMC Creative World
Pullman Road
Wigston
Leicester LE18 2DY
UK

Pioneer Patches
Marsh Mills
Luck Lane
Huddersfield
Yorkshire HD3 4AB
UK

Threadbear Supplies
11 Northway
Deanshanger
Milton Keynes MK19 6NF
UK
(waddings/battings)

DMC Corporation
Port Kearny
Building 10
South Kearny
New Jersey 07032
USA

P & B Fabrics
898 Mahler Road
Burlingame
California 94010
USA

DMC Needlecraft
PO Box 317
Earlwood
NSW 2206
Australia

Auckland Folk Art Centre
591 Remuera Road
Remuera
Auckland
New Zealand

The Craft Lady
47 Bramley Gardens
Corlett Drive
Bramley
Johannesburg
South Africa

MOSAIC SUPPLIES

Edgar Udny & Co Ltd
The Mosaic Centre
83–85 Bondway
London SW8 1SQ
UK

Reed Harris Ltd
Riverside House
Carnwath Road
London SW6 3HS
UK

Mosaic Crafts Inc
80 West Street
New York
New York 10012
USA

Camden Art Centre Pty Ltd
188–200 Gertrude Street
Fitzroy
Victoria 3065
Australia

CONTRIBUTORS

Vicki Ambery-Smith
4 Melgund Road
London N5 1PT

Amanda Barry
17 Barber Close
Winchmore Hill
London N21 1BE

Rosalind Beardshaw
7 Brooklands Drive
Sheffield S10 49H

Jan Bridge
c/o the Publishers

Marion Elliot
9 Huddlestone Road
London N7 0AE

Deidre Hawken and
Gudren Luckett
35 Glenluce Road
London SE23 7SD

Jill Hancock
Harbour Studios
Porlock Weir
Minehead
Somerset TA24 8PD

Nicola Henshaw
4011/2 Workshops
Wandsworth Road
London SW8 2JP

Kim Jeffries
56A Lincoln Road
Peterborough PE1 2RY

Rachel Maidens
51 Devonshire Drive
North Anston, Nr Sheffield
Yorkshire S31 7AN

Christopher and Susan Mather
Mistletoe Cottage
Copmere End, Eccleshall
Staffordshire ST21 6HH

Linda McVeigh
c/o Publishers

Abigail Mill
Studio 10, Muspole Workshops
25–27 Muspole Street
Norwich, Norfolk NR3 1DJ

Linda Miller
Abbots Barton Farmhouse
Abbots Barton, Winchester
Hampshire SO2 37HY

Sarah Moorman
32 Windrush Road
Keynsham, Bristol BS18 1ED

Ann Marie Mulligan
c/o the Publishers

Julie Nock
3 Elcho Court
Altrincham
Cheshire WA14 2TB

Sarah Parker Eaton
29 Morrell Close
Luton
Bedfordshire LU3 3XB

Trisha Rafferty
54 Byron Street
Brighton BN3 5BB

Kisty Rees
Caerwigua Isaf
Pedoylan, Cowbridge
South Wales

Katie Scampton
c/o Publishers

Emma Whitfield
3 Tressider House
Clapham Park Estate
Poynders Road
London SW4 8PU

ACKNOWLEDGEMENTS

*The author and publishers would like
to thank the following companies for
supplying items for photography:*

Antiques and Things
91 Eccles Road
London SW11

Crocodile Leap
16 Bellevue Road
London SW17

Tessa Fantoni
24 Abbeville Road
London SW17

General Trading Company
144 Sloane Street
London SW1

Janik Woodcrafts
Brickfield Lane
Denbigh Road
Ruthin, Wales

Lucky Parrot
2 Bellevue Road
London SW17

Mosaic Workshop
46 Elburne Road
London N7

The Pavillion
22b Bellevue Road
London SW17

The Shaker Shop
25 Harcourt Street
London W1

Stitches and Daughters
5–7 Tranquil Vale
London SE3

*Thanks are due to the following
individuals for loaning their own
boxes.* The Ashford family, Ann
Broadbent, Sasha Haworth, the

Holstrom family, V J Lowe,
Helen Moulton, Mike Moxley,
Ray Moxley and Ann Scampton,
Michelle Pelley, Jill Sheridan and
John Haworth, Barbara
Stoddard, Netty Turner.

*The author and Publishers would also
like to thank* Pandouro Hobby
Ltd, West Way House, Transport
Avenue, Brentford, Middlesex
TW8 9HF, (tel: 081 847 6161),
*for the supply of plain wooden boxes
used in the projects.*

INDEX